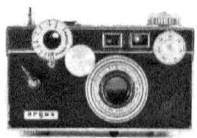

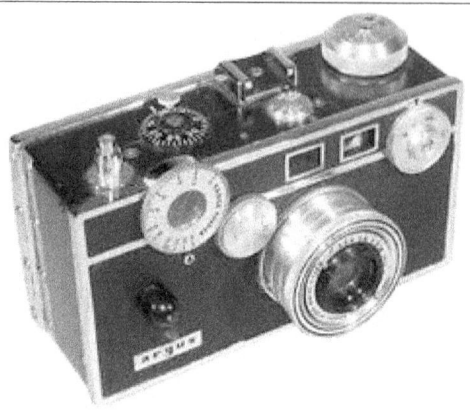

DoubleExposure
DoubleTrouble

In this novella by
Richard Everett
Londgren...

Haste Makes Waste
and complications...during a
photography assignment

Copyright 2015

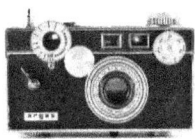

CHAPTERS

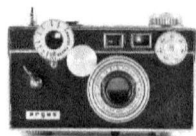

FOREWORD

When I shopped for my first camera, the black, boxy Argus C3, with its chrome accents, caught my eye.

After all, I had only used a Box Brownie before.

Others encouraged me to get this low-cost 35mm, with its array of appealing features. Of course, they didn't alert me about some of its limitations until after I had bought the Black Beauty.

Fortunately, I also had signed up for a photography class. Others in the class encouraged me, emphasizing the plusses and helping me cope with the minuses.

So I learned how to compensate for challenges such as lighting and movement. Then I used a tripod to deal with light and steadiness. And I learned the C3's lack of precise flash synchronization limited night sports-action photography.

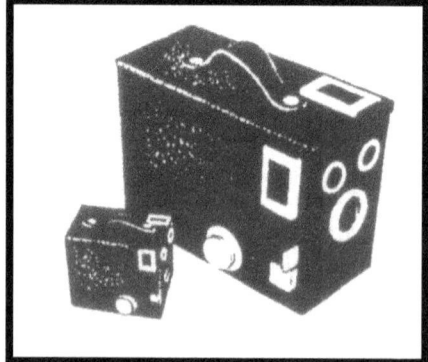

Later, I used other 35mm's, press cameras, twin-lens reflexes, and now digital cameras. I don't want to give away my story, so I will say no more about the nature and functions of the various cameras.

Along the way, however, I did create this Box Brownie enlargement, so to speak.

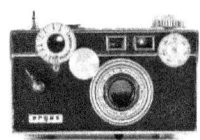

I made a large plywood mail box as shown in the photo, at the right of the smaller actual Box Brownie. The enlarged box features a variety of chrome pieces and a leather strap to simulate that historic camera.

(That photo and explanation also appear in my self-published book, *Poor Richard's TIPS from the Great Depression.* That hand-assembled edition—with covers printed by me on my antique platen press—is available directly from me, or get a digital version via Amazon's Kindle.)

Alas, now digital cameras have replaced the old favorites. On the other hand, no more film-developing, contact prints, enlargers, 35-mm slide projectors.

But I do at least "picture" the prospect of installing a digital camera inside a Box Brownie case.

Cool! Wouldn't that get attention!

Richard Everett Londgren

Meanwhile, enjoy this story—as told via student
Sarah Karlstrom

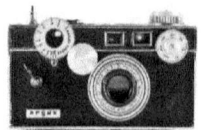

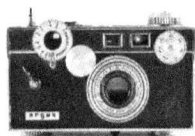

Chapter 1: Photography 101

When my cousin **Janet Karlstrom** came to visit me in Redwood City before she headed off to college, we chuckled as we talked about our high school life we just finished.

We also laughed when folks in town couldn't tell us apart. Like two peas in a pod. At my church and hers, others were often puzzled. We looked alike, even dressed in the same trendy way for the time.

No, I smiled in my church, I'm **Sarah Karlstom**, from here, and she's my cousin Janet, who lives not far from here in Mountain View.

BACKGROUND BRIEFING

Sarah's community of Redwood City, California is a small city in the southern part of the San Francisco Bay area. The name reflects a characteristic of the area, as does nearby and similar-sized Mountain View, home of her cousin Janet.

In 1946, we both had just graduated from high school. Hard to believe what the world had been through, as we talked about the end of the war last year.

Though Janet and I, and our families, had comfy lives in the enjoyable climate and environment of California, we often talked about the terrible changes associated with the war, including the death of President Roosevelt, the atomic bomb that finally brought the war against Japan to a close, and the current painful recovery occurring around the world.

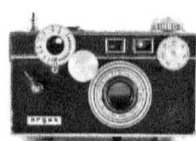

We enjoyed getting an occasional "wolf whistle" or the popular line "Hey good-lookin', what cha got cookin'?"

On weekends, when our music, drama and sports schedules had allowed, the two of us got together by taking the train. Not like some young people who hitch-hiked. Maybe okay for boys, but not for us. Besides gas rationing limited traffic and chances for a ride anyway.

Soldiers in uniform had the best luck in catching rides. That related to the ongoing discussions about the pressure to bring home the troops, while the new United Nations sought to control the uneasy peace.

Our parents worried about that and the many other challenges facing President Truman after he moved up from Vice President. For many reasons, the President had to resist the public clamor to bring the troops home immediately. For a practical transition from wartime to peacetime, he had to stall the public demand for elimination of a variety of government controls.

Meanwhile, by going back and forth by train, Janet and I got together without worry about running out of gas. Neither of us has a steady boyfriend, so our socializing generally depends on local activities with our friends.

So several of us did appreciate a recent movie favorite, *Casablanca.*

Various scenes reminded us to be thankful that the war was finally over. We liked the local angle—that the hanger at the Van Nuys airport in southern California was where the movie's conclusion had been filmed.

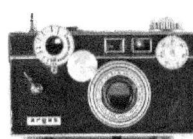

What to do next? we sometimes wondered. Maybe we should just decide to do as Claude Rains might say—round up the usual friends and make our own fun.

Though Janet and I looked forward to college, we also agreed we had a good time in high school. Even learned a lot!

I added that I particularly learned from my special role as writer-photographer for the school newspaper.

Then I told Janet about my unusual assignment to write a story and take photos of our school's auto-shop class. Interesting and challenging. The all-boys class treated me like a celebrity, because our paper had never written about them before.

The class instructor offered his personal appreciation when he learned that the school newspaper planned to run a series—not just one story—about the auto-shop program.

He jokingly called me *Brenda Starr, Reporter*, after the comic strip by that name. I countered—make that *Sarah Karlstrom, Photo-Journalist,* because I take photos as well as write my stories.

But, as Brenda Starr might respond, I added a warning to the auto-shop class that I'd learned to be tough, so don't you mechanics try to pull the wool over my eyes. Besides, I let them know that my dad and brother know plenty about cars and would check my stories.

One brash student interrupted: At least I vote that you're as good looking as Brenda Starr. Several others agreed, so then I was the subject of some wolf-whistles and an undercurrent of howls as the students expressed their opinions.

But the class did let me know their shared complaint about fairness.

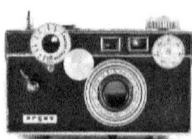

"I think it's high time the school paper recognized us!" shouted one student. "We're sick of being treated as second-class citizens, just because we have dirt under our fingernails and wear coveralls!"

Legitimate beef, I agreed, so I got his name and jotted his comment in my notebook. Hang on, I said, as I got my camera ready for action and took his picture.

Then the instructor reminded the students to be prepared to explain and show the repair projects underway. And tell Miss Karlstrom why you think our auto-shop course is an important part of the education program here.

Cousin Janet laughed when I explained that the shop students also like to get sympathy for their skinned knuckles, just as athletes want for their bruises.

BACKGROUND BRIEFING

Unlike schools in many other countries, technical training had been given a back seat in much of America, despite the vast industrial complex of the country. Partly because of the electronics evolution during and after World War II, and the change in the work force, the education system has responded.

Your good looks obviously got their attention too, laughed Janet.

Yes, as a matter of fact, I warned them that flattery would get them nowhere—though I admit enjoyed it.

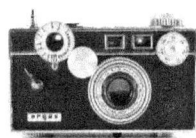

Did they inquire, Janet wondered, whether you could be their pin-up babe, like the posters I've seen in gas stations?

Not yet, but I guess that might go with my glamour image, I laughed.

In a way, I explained, I sort of "joined" the class.

But it was hands on, hands dirty—with hand dexterity required.

Of course, some of those young guys tended to brush up against me as I helped make a simple repair such as changing a light bulb or adding water to a radiator. That, of course, was just part of their desire to teach me about basic mechanics.

Naturally, laughed Janet, as she admitted that the class sounds like fun. Let me know when you need someone to carry your camera bag. I wouldn't mind a little brushing up.

Well, I explained to Janet, to do justice to the story, I did have to go back to the class several times. Surprisingly, I found the training and actual repair work to be interesting. Even had a chance to test-drive one fancy car that had been jazzed up by the class.

In later discussion over dinner at home with my parents, I continued my report as I shared details about my journalism assignment.

The class intrigued Dad. Even Mom...a bit.

They, of course, saw the humor of the instructor comparing me to Brenda Starr, Reporter. And Mom and Dad liked my response that the class should consider me "Sarah Karlstrom, Photo-Journalist."

Then my report about the paint shop certainly got Dad's attention, as I told about seeing an array of DuPont labels on the shelves. Dad

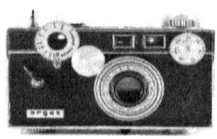

laughed when Mom accused me of using paint as a way to get accepted by the class.

Well, I explained, I did tell about your work, Dad. Even said that you might be willing to visit the class and tell about the special characteristics of paint.

Sarah sure "painted you into a corner," laughed Mom.

That's our Sarah, she added. So, Jim, do you think you can boil down your chemistry to help explain car paint?

Guess I'll have to think back to my high school days and focus on the basics. Could be interesting. Could encourage more students—boys and girls—to include practical training in their mix of studies.

By the way, how did your camera work? asked Dad. Any more double-exposures?

Just one, I admitted. Got in a hurry when I changed lenses and forgot to advance the film.

But I may have been lucky. Next I shot a close-up of Ron Hanson—

BACKGROUND BRIEFING

The Argus C3 being used by Sarah was a popular American-made 35mm camera of the '30s and quite a while later with improved models. Besides being low-cost, it featured regular, close-up and wide-angle interchangeable lenses. A range-finder helped with the focus and an indicated exposure time related to approximate light level. Unfortunately, the flash wasn't synchronized accurately, so the camera had to be set at a slow speed to catch the light from a flash bulb. And the Argus didn't automatically require film advancement, hence the possible double-exposures.

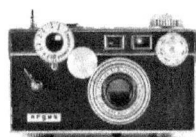

you probably recognize his name from church. A smart but quiet guy who was in my confirmation class.

Anyway, I intentionally double-exposed a close-up of him combined with the shop in the background. Could be interesting. But I might have to do some extra work in our darkroom to make the double-exposure into a good photo.

Then I told Mom and Dad about a different challenge. Taking a photo of the Girls' Glee Club—with me in it.

So I set up the camera on my tripod and composed the group photo. Then I asked another nearby student to snap the photo with the attached cable release…after I dashed to get in my place.

Now, I announced, the darkroom will "expose the truth," as Dad and Mom laughed at the pun.

Remember, Mom reminded me, turn on the fan and don't stay in the darkroom too long before coming out for a breath of fresh air.

I agree, long exposure to those chemicals could be harmful, confirmed Dad.

By the way, Dad, I still have that strip of negatives hanging in our darkroom to warn me that the Argus doesn't automatically advance the film.

And that certainly reminds me that my accidental double-exposure during the parade wasn't the best way to show my skills to our community newspaper staff.

Yeah, you could say that again! laughed Dad.

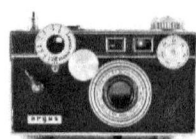

Later, when Janet and I got together again for coffee, she complimented me about my photo-journalism coverage of the auto-shop class. I heard you won an award for that story! she exclaimed.

Well, eventually my faux-Kodak proved itself, with its three lenses, I explained. Both the wide-angle and the close-up helped me get the variety of photos. Changing lenses is a bit awkward. But I even remembered to advance the film as called for—most of the time. Still, haste sure can make waste—though I only double-exposed a couple of the photos I snapped.

Good one! laughed Janet. Snappy admission. No pun intended.

Then I told her about meeting the notorious Stan Logan in the shop class. I explained that he declared to me right out that he likes good looks in cars—and girls. Including me.

Well, Stan Logan—and his glitzy car—did dazzle me, briefly. Like a shooting star, I confessed to Janet. But I did pay attention when one of the other students warned me about "Slick & Sleazy Stan."

Oh, the plot thickens! chuckled Janet, with more than a hint of curiosity.

Maybe his hope to pick you up will perk me up, she added. Recover from the letdown I felt at graduation. Maybe for you, too, with college concerns distracting from your honors.

She admitted her own angst. She felt that her graduation speech must have flopped, because she lacked the spirit for it.

I hope you can line me up this summer with an interesting boyfriend, who only looks like Stan. With a cute car, of course. With me in it, laughed Janet.

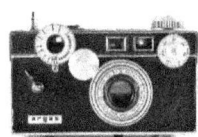

Dream on about that kind of guy, I scoffed. And the cute car too. Stan soon revealed himself as only half cute and half smart. And I was a fool to be impressed, even if momentarily.

Guess I was too self-centered to bother with Ron Hanson, the smartest guy in our class. Mister nice guy. Helped me with science. Helped me in the school photo lab. Helped me with the Argus C3 Dad got for me.

The practical C3 came with Dad's reminder, of course—that for some things, "Good enough is good enough."

Even so, my camera gets attention. Its handsome squarish design gets praise. Stylish, with black Bakelite accented by chrome.

And, well, I have to admit, cool means a lot to me.

Yeah, I know, agreed Janet. Look sharp, not be smart.

In stretch of camera comparison, I guess you'd say that a "flash in the pan" sort of guy lacks "depth of field."

Maybe you would say that, not me, laughed Janet, as she tolerated my attempt at a metaphor. Or simile?

I admitted to Janet another reason I should have paid more attention to Ron. He's building a Hot Rod as part of the latest car trend for young guys. He is smart and skilled, but at that earlier time, he didn't seem sophisticated enough for me. Now I learned that he has even written an article for a proposed new magazine about Hot Rods. So when he asked me if I would take some photos for his story, I had declined with the excuse that I was just too busy…trying to make sense of myself. I hope I'll get another chance.

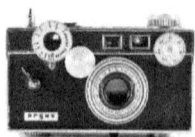

My brother Bill would hope for that too. He had reminded me to beware of jerks like "Stan the Con Man." He recalled that even when they played marbles as kids, Stan would cheat by shifting his "shooter" closer to the pot if he got a chance. He'd also swipe candy, other things. Had to watch him. If he got caught, he'd try to lie his way out of it. Now, added Bill, he's still seems to be the smooth talker, too lazy to study or work. But he turns on his charm with anybody he wants to influence.

Don't even trust his cute cars, warned Bill. His patched-up fancy cars might not even be legal for driving, he explained.

How's that? asked Janet, who had been all ears about my tales of woe.

Well, Bill wonders about Stan's shyster Logan family—and their shady car and implement business. Involved in the Black Market, he emphasized. They scour the whole area to get scarce stuff cheap to fix up and cover up and sell for a big profit to eager farmers and others during and after the war.

Bill suspects that the Logans have even changed identifications on damaged cars, patched up the bodies and repainted them. But he suspects that they've paid little attention to such basics as brakes and steering.

Maybe Bill will be able to pursue that kind of deception after he starts a law internship or later gets his law degree.

Bill admitted his own prejudice about the Logans, and that he and his football pals have always disliked and distrusted Stan. He says they would like to pound that smug crook into the ground.

I appreciate Bill's protectiveness. And his talent and determination. Paid off for him. He gets a full ride at Stanford for being smart…

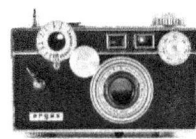

and a great football player. He lets me know that I can win too, if I "stay focused"…as he laughed at his own pun.

You're a good athlete yourself, Janet reminded me.

Maybe not disciplined enough to be outstanding as an athlete, I admitted. But I did enjoy being a cheerleader.

I told Janet she could soon meet Stan. He's going to be involved in a community event I've been assigned to cover.

Want to come along?

Wouldn't miss it! Janet exclaimed.

Then you can judge for yourself, I said. Talk to Stan like you're interviewing him. Then he'll be super sweet and brag his head off.

With him, keep in mind this saying: Fool me once, shame on you; fool me twice, shame on me!

Is that a metaphor, like staying focused? Or a simile? I asked with a wry smile.

Never could keep those straight, laughed Janet, as we both laughed.

Anyway, I guess I really shouldn't connect you in any with Stan, I admitted.

I don't want to repeat an earlier mistake, I said, as I explained that I had introduced Stan at a previous community event to one of my classmates. Her beauty appealed to him. And she was taken in by his bravado…and his expensive clothes….and his spending money…and his fancy convertible.

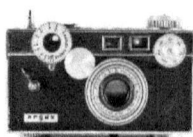

Fills me with guilt, I conceded, because, tragically, she died while driving one of his fancy cars. She lost control and was thrown out of the car, which rolled on top of her.

At least, Stan showed some remorse about her death. He said he was sorry that he had gone out of town the day she drove his car, first in a parade in town and then she rolled it over on the highway.

But, as a photographer covering that event for our community newspaper, I still have a lingering feeling that Stan was in the background when I took Stacy's photo before the parade that day.

He denied he was there, as he explained that he had left long before the parade to take in an auction of farm equipment over by Fresno. His dad had sent him to bid on a tractor and combine. Didn't buy, he said—too rich for our blood. No profit margin for us, he had explained.

But my haunting memory made me suspicious of him. Though I checked the photos I took that day, I couldn't find him in the photos. Because my haste and the camera's manual film advance, I had double-exposed twice that day. So I glanced at the messed up negatives, but saw no obvious sign of him there either. So I pushed that out of my brain.

At least Stan avoids talking to me now. But he's snagged another cutie from our class. Still, when I tried to warn her about his style, she just laughed at me and called me jealous and vengeful.

What's this? Janet asked suddenly, as if she had come out of a daze about my reference to the car wreck.

Sorry that I didn't pick up on the significance of your photography, she admitted. And the tragic accident. Suddenly it dawned on me—you really are a professional photographer!

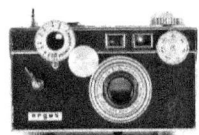

Yup, sort of, I answered. I learned from Dad and our school photography club and class. So recently I advanced to photographer for our community newspaper as well as high school paper.

That's why I'm scheduled to take some photos of a sports-car rally that Stan's in. He has one of those half-size cars, I added sarcastically.

Now, urged Janet, fill me in more about your career in photography. No wonder you're winning awards, by the sound of it.

Well, I answered, I am basically a photographer getting on-the-job training, I admitted. At school. At home, too. As you know, Dad works as a chemist for DuPont, so he helped me set up a darkroom at home to develop film and make prints. With her art background, Mom encourages me to think of composition, lighting and variations in focus. It's fun and challenging, provides me a sense of independence. Need that to salvage my reputation as sometimes superficial and to regain some respect from my classmates.

Besides, I get paid by our newspaper. Not much. But I do get some perks. Free admission to some interesting events. Meet a few big shots. People at events flatter me with hope I'll take their picture.

Also, this adds to my hope for work-study and college scholarships.

You probably know, it's getting tougher just to get accepted by a college. Colleges are crowded, with so many former soldiers and sailors packing the schools with their GI Bill to pay their way.

Officially, I explained when Janet seemed puzzled, the actual name for the GI Bill experiment is the Servicemen's Readjustment Act of 1944.

So, have you applied at a specific college for yourself? she asked.

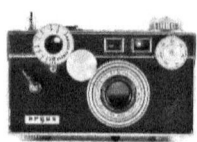

Santa Barbara College. It's an expanding part of the state system. Still small, so I might have a chance to participate in student activities. I plan to study chemistry like Dad. Maybe some art like Mom. Fortunately, I got a partial DuPont scholarship.

How about you? I asked Janet.

I'm off to Humboldt State, to study forestry. A long way from you but close enough to see each other once in a while.

Lots of soldiers there too. But I got an academic scholarship related to my interest in science.

BACKGROUND BRIEFING

In a Mediterranean-like atmosphere along the Pacific Coast of Southern California, Santa Barbara claims Spanish heritage for its name. During World War II, military installations dominated the community, and some of those bases were converted to be part of the evolving state university. Santa Barbara also notes the distinction of being the only community in the United States shelled by a Japanese submarine during the war.

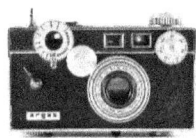

Chapter 2: Ground Glass and Viewfinder

As I pondered my next photo assignment, I thought about photography in our family. Our involvement goes back to 1926 when Dad served as the photographer for the student newspaper at Augustana College in Rock Island, Illinois.

The newspaper's need fit my father's interest. Besides, he was studying chemistry, so that related to processing film and making prints. And that justified the college's creating and equipping a darkroom to support his press camera—a Kodak Box Brownie. He had to deal with limitations of that simple camera—sometimes setting up flood lights because the Brownie had no flash attachment, of course.

He graduated just before the Great Depression, and I was born about then too. Shortly after Bill. Despite the tough times, DuPont saw the writing on the wall—or saw the war on the wall. So the company recruited Dad to help add to the company's variety of products—particularly explosives. The draft board realized his work at DuPont was more valuable than military service.

Eventually, with the help of more training, experience and equipment, he advanced rapidly to a higher level in the company. And advanced in his hobby of photography too.

During the war, he acquired a used Graflex press camera. Heavy, capable...but complicated. Set the speed and lens opening as indicated by separate light meter. Next, focus on a ground-glass viewer on the back. Shift as necessary to compose and to adapt to the available light. Then focus. Add a flash bulb if necessary.

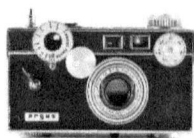

Finally, insert the film holder, pull out the film cover plate and click the shutter for the exposure.

No wonder I got confused and messed up occasionally as I went through those steps.

To simplify his teaching, Dad created a pinhole camera out of a cigar box that could hold a sheet of film like he used in his Graflex. He pierced the box with a needle and covered the hole until he was ready to expose the film. Then he aimed at the subject and held the box secure and allowed a few minutes for exposure. Finally, he opened the box in the darkroom and processed the film and made a print.

Impressive! I recalled.

As a chemist, Dad had helped set up a photo lab in our high school and taught special classes in photography. Naturally, he and Mom teamed up to provide individual instruction for my brother and me. Mom also applied photography in teaching art in high school. For show and tell, Dad also demonstrated camera technology with three damaged German war souvenirs he had acquired from returning soldiers—a 35mm Leica, a twin-lens Rolleiflex and a Minox spy camera. To use his salvaged Leica, he replaced the damaged lens with a pinhole cover. Used the light meter to determine the length of exposure. Got some great results with that weird combination.

Our family also visited the camera obscura exhibit below the Cliff House restaurant in San Francisco. Strange, standing inside that giant camera. The panoramic scene appeared on a table for viewing. With her interest in art, Mom explained how the amazing Leonardo Da Vinci created his own camera obscura.

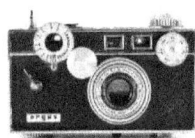

Our school newspaper staff initially bumbled along with Dad's well-worn Graflex press camera. And for simplicity, a Box Brownie, of course. But Dad had his eye on some 35mm cameras by Kodak. Though much lower priced than the foreign cameras, they still exceeded the budget of our school newspaper.

Then he learned about a popular, affordable American 35mm camera. Uses roll film, not the plates to insert and then flip over for the second shot.

Stop me if you've heard enough about the Argus C3 he got. Compact, durable and attractive, it features the interchangeable lenses, I mentioned. A range-finder assists with focusing. But it requires use of a light meter to coordinate shutter speed and exposure settings.

With it, I can supplement available light with flash bulbs and flood lights. But the lens and flash aren't precisely synchronized. So I have to select a slow shutter-speed setting to fit the duration of the light. And often that produces blurred action scenes—unless light and luck combine to create suitable photos. But it does produce some artistic effects at times—usually accidental.

And one simple limitation of the C3 certainly can cause problems.

It did for me. The shutter doesn't lock after a shot to ensure the film has been advanced. Forget that step and you would get a double exposure—like it or not.

And that happened to me when I was covering that community event. So I keep that on display in our darkroom at home as a visual reminder to advance the film on the C3.

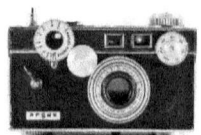

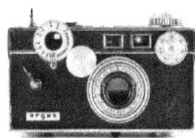

Chapter 3: Off to My College

I had pre-registered at Santa Barbara College by phone and mail and was accepted—with a financial arrangement including my DuPont scholarship for room, board, books and fees. The college also offered me the opportunity to get paid for working in the college photo department. Thanks to the state of California, I owed no tuition.

I planned to stay in a dormitory to start, but with hope for acceptance later in a sorority. That option is just evolving, because the college has grown recently from a normal school for teachers. But I continue to think of myself as a glamour-puss, deserving such special treatment. Still, I decided not to try out for cheerleading. Sour grapes. From what I learned, the cheer squad doesn't seem that great at Santa Barbara. And I should have plenty on my plate without that.

BACKGROUND BRIEFING

After high-school graduation in 1946, Sarah didn't think she could qualify for the University of California at Berkeley or for Stanford. But the scientific emphasis at a California technical school in San Luis Obispo appealed to her. Alas and surprisingly, that college did not accept female students. So she shifted her sights to the state college in Santa Barbara. As a former teachers' college, it did accept women.

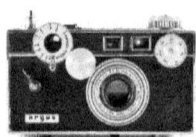

Our whole gang, James my dad, Christine my mom, Bill my brother, and me, drove down in our 1941 luxurious Buick Roadmaster.

Good choice of car, explains Dad, especially because DuPont maintains a close link with General Motors. Makes a good impression when he consults with DuPont clients, he emphasizes.

What a luxury this is, said Mom, to drive—when ample gas is available. Good thing we could ride the trains during the war.

Hard to realize that the Golden Gate Bridge opened only about ten years ago, she added. And to think that both that and the Bay Bridge were built during the Great Depression.

The trauma of the war made that decade seem like forever, she said.

Yeah, said Dad, during the war we only got an allocation of three gallons of gas a week. Our Buick is powerful, so it uses a powerful amount of gas.

At least, he laughed, we didn't drive enough to wear out our tires. Tires were rationed too.

When we went by San Simeon, Mom took advantage of her captive audience to talk about art. The Hearst Castle here, she explained, serves as an example of art collections by the rich. Don't know if they like the art or just like to show off the art. And get a tax deduction. Maybe if we drive your direction again, Sarah, we will get a chance stop and see for ourselves.

Now, we benefit from lots of art in San Francisco. Including the photography by Ansel Adams.

Certainly an inspiration for me, I stated.

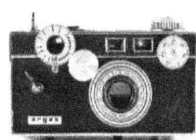

We all admired the changing terrain. Flat, mountainous, brush-covered hills.

Great for the artist's easel, declared Mom. When I studied art at Augustana, we sure didn't have any mountains to paint. On the other hand, so to speak, we did learn from our noted regional artist Grant Wood that the hills of the Midwest could be inspiring.

That well-tended Iowa farmland left little opportunity for a fire, said Dad. Not the case here. The wild plants on the rugged hills and mountains thrive after the spring rain. Then they dry up to become tinder for raging fires.

BACKGROUND BRIEFING

The early Spanish named many Saints in California, from San (male) Francisco to Santa (female) Barbara. In between, several other places such as San Luis Obispo, Santa Maria, Santa Paula.... And mountain ranges such as San Gabriel, Santa Lucia, Santa Monica...plus the San Andreas earthquake fault.

Maybe now, he speculated, our surplus bombers can be converted to become flying fire trucks. New chemicals might help fight fires too.

When I was in college, he continued, we heard about many forest fires. Killed hundreds of people in a town in northern Minnesota. Even worse in parts of Washington and Oregon. California too.

Sad to hear about, said Bill. Not over yet either, I imagine. Even threatens the Redwoods, I suppose.

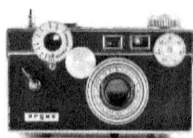

And our earthquakes sure won't let us get complacent about nature, Dad added.

Then, as we drove by Camp Roberts, about half-way to Santa Barbara, we were all startled by the military gear stacked everywhere. Khaki-clad soldiers all over the place, too, just lounging around if they weren't marching. Passing the time till they got out. Dad reminded us that now the Army focuses on winding down after the war, with lots of surplus equipment to process. And lots of men—and some women—to be released from their military duty.

A lot of that had been accumulated for shipment to the Pacific front, explained Mom.

Now even the Jeep, said Dad, has converted to peacetime, with Willys manufacturing a civilian version. Some farmers have discovered its four-wheel-drive advantages and its alternative tractor-like lower range in the transmission. Even offers a power takeoff option for operating special attachments.

Here might be a surprise to you, Christine, added Dad. Then he reported that he had just learned that the art community has recognized the simple design of the Jeep. The Museum of Modern Art has honored it as a masterpiece of functional design.

Well, DuPont has shifted gears, too, he added. Now turning to commercial applications of products, several of which DuPont had developed as part of the war effort. Fabrics, foods, films and fertilizers, as well as a myriad of chemicals and explosives. He explained that he would also be shifting to a focus of advising about newer applications of the DuPont products, resources and research. He admitted he feels challenged to keep track of all the improvements and new developments.

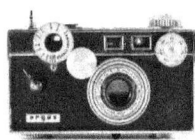

When we went through the appealing community of San Luis Obispo, Dad talked about the importance of the technology training at the college there. He remarked that the college is growing, mainly from a swarm of veterans enrolling through the GI Bill. Now it includes a small city of barracks-like housing for the military veterans at the campus.

Along the way, even more military surpluses shocked us. We agreed that it almost looks like the American military is preparing for another invasion.

Strange, Mom reflected about the colleges, that women still could not enroll at California Polytechnic University at San Luis Obispo despite the advancement in women's rights, especially in California. Probably excludes even women military veterans.

Ironically, the school did have a *Rosie the Riveter* program to train women for jobs during the war, but the female involvement ended with the end of the war.

Well, our Founding Fathers left out women's rights, too, she declared. Took a long time just to get the right to vote, she added. Maybe we should have had some Founding Mothers involved in the original planning.

BACKGROUND BRIEFING

Susan B. Anthony and Elizabeth Cady Stanton were key advocates for voting rights for women. The drive led to the 19th Amendment to the U.S. Constitution in 1920. The significance of women during World War I also influenced change.

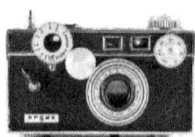

At least this current invasion in education, Dad surmised, should result in important advancement in understanding the scope of our country as well as a great leap in learning for a whole generation.

Mom echoed his conclusion, as she exclaimed that our country has endorsed a new Declaration of Independence by offering hope and opportunity for all—women included this time, she emphasized. But not at all campuses, even though California considers itself on the cutting edge of change.

That war-worker *Rosie the Riveter*, from Alameda near us, who proved to be an inspiration in industry—was later not only excluded from colleges such as Cal Poly, but Rosie will probably soon be out of work as industry slows down and male veterans take over jobs.

All the same, said Bill, this revolution serves women in most colleges, even though that opportunity lags behind the progressiveness of Stanford.

Dad had arranged to meet a friend and colleague in the Santa Barbara chemistry department. Probably for several purposes. To get an insider's insights about the change in the student body, to share some of his hopes expected for DuPont, and perhaps to give me an edge in my study of chemistry.

We also got a taste of the cuisine of the dining hall, and my mother pronounced it ample, edible and healthy.

Naturally, we noticed quite a cluster of older male students. Some still in khaki.

Even a few older women in the group—and Bill concluded that they look hearty and healthy—and attractive. I hope you can provide me an ongoing report about them, he challenged me—with a grin.

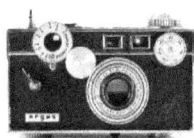

Chapter 4: Contrasts and Connections

When I called home after a few days, I got the third-degree with questions. Yes, I reported, I appreciate the three other women in my room. Diverse interests, with me the only one planning a science major. The others: Music, literature, psychology. Teaching remains a significant choice for many, especially the women. We're enjoying the mix. We eat dinner together with others from the dorm. Sometimes men drop by. The military students seem quite serious compared to the younger students, so they don't join in much. But that will probably change as we get used to each other in the classroom.

My English class indicates the nature of change. The professor assigned seats alphabetically, so my neighbor's name is Keith Kragstad. One of lots and lots of veterans. We communicated enough to share that we both have Scandinavian roots. His from Nebraska to go with mine from Illinois.

I also learned that he plans to study engineering. My interest in chemistry impressed him, I believe. But he admitted that the English class scares him. Said he leans more toward handling vehicles than verbs. Directed a Motor Pool in the Army. I don't know what that is, but I am curious, considering my experience with cars. Not all good, of course.

Three others nearby in that class come from our dorm. So they're enjoying telling others about my tall and handsome boyfriend. No—he's a man-friend, not boyfriend, they declare. Hope that doesn't scare off boyfriends.

Does that answer your questions, even if you didn't get a chance to ask them?

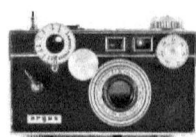

By the way, I did stop by the college photography department, and I dropped in at the student newspaper office. Talented bunch, and they welcomed me enthusiastically.

I hadn't intended to show my Argus C3, but one of the student photographers noticed it. He said the department photographers use new Kodak 35mm cameras, but he recognized that my Argus would be personally more affordable and useful. Maybe I've started a trend. Of course, I'll have to warn about the risk of double exposure. Without admitting my own film fiasco.

Well, before you sign off, said Mom, I'll just report that we're doing fine. Getting used to the empty nest, with Bill now gone much of the time for football at Stanford. We miss both of you.

Here's Dad with his part of our conversation.

Sounds like you've already found a new community, he noted, not to mention a man-friend.

Just one warning about your camera: Don't forget to take the lens cap off. And remember to advance the film.

Hey, that's two warnings!

After that, all three of us signed off with a happy laugh.

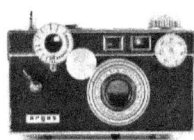

Chapter 5: Bridging Backgrounds

My roommates and others in the dorm insisted that Keith must be my man-friend. Who would pass him by? seemed to be the assumption by the others. I admit, I felt a bit that way myself, as I reflected about the difference between my past suitors—including brazen Stan—and this quiet and confident veteran of combat.

Well, maybe not so confident about English, as I smiled about his confession.

Thoughts about the veterans at school led me to inquire in our dorm: Do you know anybody in our dorm who serves on the student government?

Before getting an answer, I explained that maybe the conventional students should invite the veterans to a social gathering. Such as a table-hopping event, I mentioned, as a way for students to get acquainted.

When asked to tell more, I suggested an arrangement in which a few veterans could be stationed at each of about a dozen tables. Then the civilians, male and female, would join them. We could ring a bell after about 10 minutes. Then the civilians would move to the next table.

One of my roommates said she knew one dorm leader who also represented the dorm as part of the student government. Nothing ventured, nothing gained, she declared, as she vowed to follow up on such an inquiry.

Okay, big-mouth, I reminded myself, my idea may generate interest all the way to the student government. Now what?

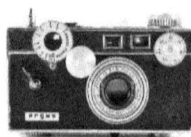

My roommates, plus others from our dorm and some male friends agreed to be a planning committee. Might be good to have a few veterans on the committee, too, we decided. So the others assigned me to broach the idea with my man-friend Keith.

Well, by this time, Keith and I had advanced to being comfortable neighbors in the classroom, slowly getting acquainted. When I suggested the table-hopping idea, he didn't hop on it, so to speak. Still, he liked it. Hard to bridge differences in age and experience, he admitted. This might be a start.

BACKGROUND BRIEFING

The U.S. military caused a major shift in American population, as implied in the World War I song, *How Ya Gonna Keep'em Down On The Farm (After They've Seen Paree?)*. Then World War II spread the troops even more. In between, the Dust Bowl of the Great Depression pushed thousands toward California, as depicted in John Steinbeck's novel and movie, *Grapes of Wrath*. Next, in the '40s, the wartime shipbuilding and aircraft industries caused more to head West.

Later, I reflected on Keith's comment about the differences he mentioned. I realized that he was only 21, even after serving in the Army during the last two years of the war. But he had also alluded to his harrowing experiences in transporting soldiers forward to confront the massive German counter-offensive near the end of the long war.

Initially in that battle, he had explained, soldiers by the truckload moved forward, feeling casual and confident, sensing an Allied

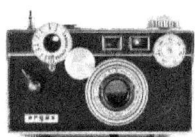

victory on the horizon, and eager to go home. Then the tide changed, when the German juggernaut overwhelmed the relaxed Allied forces.

With misty eyes, Keith grimaced as he told of desperately rounding up the isolated soldiers, hauling the wounded soldiers to the field hospital. His truck dropped off others at the staging area to regroup with their units.

Gradually, I absorbed a deeper sense of the war—and the impact on those directly involved.

The various types of rationing we endured—gasoline, shoes, foods—now seemed trivial in contrast to soldiers and sailors in battle.

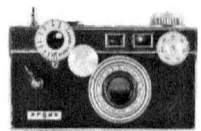

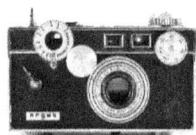

Chapter 6: Sharing the Sorrow

After I relayed my information and reactions to our committee, the others wanted more than ever to move on the plan to help the array of students to get acquainted. Each on our committee would spread the idea and seek support from a variety of contacts.

A few days later, one member of the committee caught up with me in the dorm. She said she had told her history professor about how my friend Keith had grimly reported his experience in what had become known as the Battle of the Bulge.

BACKGROUND BRIEFING

More than 17 million men and women served in the U.S. military forces during World War II. The Servicemen's Readjustment Act of 1944, called the G.I. Bill, allowed the men (and later women) to enroll in college and apply for other benefits. It has been praised in particular for the training that benefited the individuals and for the positive far-reaching impact in the United States.

The professor had mentioned that the study of history would be greatly enriched by hearing a first-hand report about such a significant conflict. So the request came to me—would I ask Keith if he would tell his story in her American history class?

I agreed to ask. But I sensed a mixed response from modest Keith, who had reacted with sorrow even when telling me about his military experiences.

Later, while we sat waiting for the professor of our English class, I asked Keith if he could spare a few minutes after class. I want to offer a proposition.

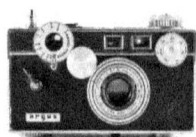

You're propositioning me, he chuckled. That does sound intriguing.

With that incentive, he offered, I'll even buy you a cup of coffee.

During the class, I saw a slight grin brightening his face. And that made me grin a bit myself. Yup, a proposition. Not the kind he might hope for. Or would I?

When he approached the table with two cups of coffee—one with cream, for me, he wore that wicked grin again. And both the coffee with cream and his grin made me smile.

He sipped his coffee. And I mine. Silence prevailed, until he asked, What do you propose?

A history lesson, I said. Then I explained the request.

That's not only a letdown, he laughed, but a scary request at that. You probably already saw how that recollection affects me. Still, he continued, in a soft way, we need to share such history. With hope it doesn't repeat.

So, he asked, will you help me develop a presentation? You know part of the story. But how could I to tell it to the young and sheltered students in that class? Mostly that type, anyway, unless the class includes some veterans.

I agreed to help, of course, because I had offered the challenge. Maybe, I thought, this too could be a way to promote the need to bridge the gap with our table-hopping event.

So I shared my thoughts about the special socializing concept of table-hopping too.

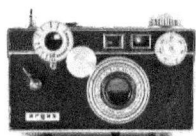

After a slow sip of coffee, to absorb the idea, he hesitantly agreed to help bridge the students. He explained that he was in charge of an Army reserve unit, so he knew several veterans who might be interested.

A good idea, he added.

Then a sudden concern came to mind. Are you married? I asked.

Why do you ask? he asked.

Well, I thought you might not want to participate in such a student event if you are.

His coffee cup was empty, but he picked it up to drink. Then he looked down, perhaps to cover tears in his eyes.

Then, quietly, he said no.

But I sensed his *no* had unsaid meaning. Maybe in due time I'd learn more.

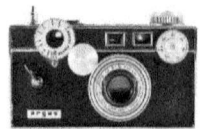

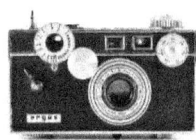

Chapter 7: Telling a Personal Story

I convinced Keith to come with me to the office of the student newspaper, called the *El Gaucho*, to seek some photography help to dramatize his presentation.

One of my fellow photographers—who's a mentor to me—mentioned that he had taken photos of a Hollywood film crew creating some stock war scenes for pending movies.

Now I remember, said Keith. They came to the Motor Pool that's part of our Army reserve unit here. I'm in charge of that. Maybe, he said to the photographer, you took photos of that wild Hollywood scene.

Yeah, and we could make slides of just the right scenes and right tone to underscore your comments. I can also check with the movie studio's publicity department for some promotional photos of the stars in action. They'd welcome that exposure.

Then editor Bob Felp of *El Gaucho* spoke up. Great ideas. This ought to wake up the class to recent history. We'll be interested in a story about your presentation. What you have to say. How the students—and professor—react. The local newspaper might be interested too.

Then I mentioned the student council's plan to have a table-hopping social event to connect the younger students with the veterans. Tell me more, said the editor.

I think we have a bigger story, he responded. About the impact of the government program to help veterans with their education. And

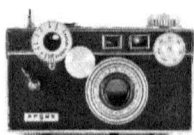

what that means to the future of the country, as well as the present impact on our campus.

Later, in a repeated coffee-break conference with Keith, I served this time, as I noted he was absorbed in thought.

I'm overwhelmed, he said, to start our conference. You overwhelm me. I'm amazed at how you could have engineered all this.

Engineered. Good term from someone who intends to become an engineer, I said. Anyway, to your question. I just seem to think that way. Analytical genes from Dad, art expression from Mom.

Now, he continued, with a subtle smile, what about that table-hopping you mentioned to the editor?

We would like to station, so to speak, about four single veterans at each of about 10 tables. Then we would send teams of two coeds and two young men to the tables for 10 minutes. Then that team would move on to the next table and another team would arrive.

Can you help?

Glad to help. And some from our reserve unit would be eager for the opportunity.

Well, you do have special selling skills, he continued. Of course, I suspect your good looks helps when you're promoting an idea.

Flattery. I like that, I said.

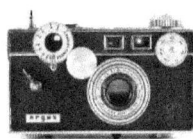

Chapter 8: From Plan to Presentation

Preparations advanced smoothly for the table-hopping, with the date set for Friday night in two weeks. No home game that weekend. No homecoming or other major conflicts.

Keith felt at ease with that. But he chewed his nails over the presentation. To practice, maybe I could orate to our trucks in the motor pool, he said. Maybe to our Jeeps. But not to a college class. Even in high school, I hardly ever spoke up.

Well, you do share plans for your unit and outline procedures with the others, don't you?

That's different.

Just imagine, sergeant—you said are—that you're reporting back to your headquarters about the consequences of the German attack.

Yeah, he said, I would need to show a truckload of happy soldiers heading toward the front. Then the misery of the wounded coming back. Explain how the Germans surprised us. Pushed us back.

Maybe Hollywood has such photos to make into slides, I reminded him.

We might seek a photo of a soldier dying in the snow. I can tell about the GI who tried to throw a grenade at a German tank, said Keith. The grenade bounced off and the tank crushed him.
I can describe the German equipment. Tell about the weather conditions. The fog that kept our planes out of the action.

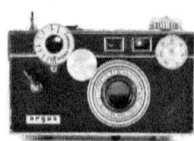

Keith continued: Not enough Medics to attend to the wounded, so we hauled them away in our trucks. We can tell about those howling in pain, crying with fear, in the field hospital.

We'll see what pictures Hollywood can provide, I assured him again.

Still, we went on planning and practicing. The *El Gaucho* photographers brought the dramatic slides promised. They brought other photos borrowed from the *San Luis Tribune* and from Hollywood. Even got posters promoting several war movies.

We can display some personal military equipment, added Keith. Rifles, machine guns and bazookas—without ammunition and guarded by our MP's—Military Police. Guess we'd better check that with campus security too.

Seems like we've got the general direction, I said. A test run or two should smooth it out.

Finally, when he entered the classroom for the presentation, Keith did look shocked. Besides a greeting from the professor, a packed room applauded to honor him. Students and professors from other classes and a few university officials had filled the room. And various reporters from local newspapers and radio stations had positioned themselves for coverage.

Then Keith began. Picture yourself in the freezing cold and blowing snow in one of the worst winters ever in Europe. Certainly not something you'd ever experience here. I was about your age, he said as he swept his arms over the audience, running our Army Motor Pool unit. According to Army standards, I had great civilian experience, because our family operated a gas station and garage in

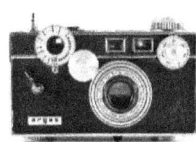

the little town of Ceresco in eastern Nebraska, near the capital, Lincoln.

In December of 1944, besides working on trucks and Jeeps inside our huge Quonset building, we were getting ready for Christmas. Look at the happy bunch in this snapshot. We were decorating a big Christmas tree, rescued from a nearby cemetery. We, like the rest of our Army unit, had been lulled into waiting for the end of the war. But suddenly for us, Christmas didn't come, but Hell did.
The war roared back.

BACKGROUND BRIEFING

Complacent near the end of the war, the Allied troops were suddenly fighting for their territory and their lives in the face of a huge counter-attack by German forces. The Battle of the Bulge left lasting shock and sorrow for Keith Kragstad and thousands of other American GI's—thankful to have survived while mourning the loss of others. Many now were striving to rebuild their lives.

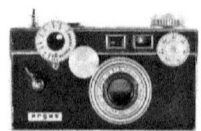

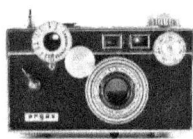

Chapter 9: Driven Back

Those of you who have read about this cataclysmic event a couple of years ago, said Keith, may recall the scope of it.

Our country had to commit a half-million troops, plus more from our Allies, to save our victory. This map shows why it was called the Battle of the Bulge, as the Germans pushed our defense back toward Antwerp.

Everything seemed to work against us. Complacency, the wearing magnitude of our war effort, and the bad weather that left us without our aerial scouting.

I still wake up shaking and in a sweat dreaming about our 20,000 dead and four times that many wounded. Our truck and Jeep drivers, me included, helped the overworked Medics. Not too carefully. Sometimes we just had to load the wounded and haul them on a rough road to our field hospital. Screaming and groaning.

We beat the enemy back, he concluded, or I wouldn't be here today.

From my continuing sadness, I share with you my sorrow that my best friend didn't make it back. As a nurse, Karina went to help the Medics…but was killed while treating a wounded soldier.

After Keith wiped away his tears, he said simply, I hope you learned more about our history…from our history…and why I hope it doesn't repeat that way.

After extended applause mixed with scattered sobbing and nose-blowing, Keith thanked them and offered to answer questions.

Why? asked a young woman. My father died in the war. Why?

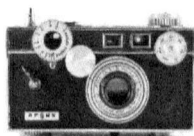

The contradictions in human behavior, I guess, answered Keith. But he admitted that he'd have to leave that up to philosophers and theologians.

And historians, as he turned to the history professor.

In response, she came forward, with tears in her eyes, to thank Keith…and the others who helped all of us witness this tragic part of history.

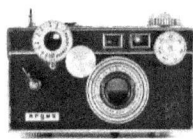

Chapter 10: Sharing the Past

In our English class, both Keith and I seemed wiped out from effort and emotion related to his Battle of the Bulge presentation.

But the professor of this class called attention to us, particularly Keith.

You showed admirable strength and commendable choice of words in telling us about the Battle of the Bulge, she said. Your graphics added immensely.

Those in the English class who had attended led brief applause. After the class, I mentioned that the *El Gaucho* staff planned to comment about the presentation and consider how to cover the topic further. I'll be there tonight. Hope you will too, Keith.

Sure will. And thanks, he said, as he started to shake hands…but hugged me instead.

Coming from him, I considered that a great honor.

Sorry about your loss of Karina, I added quietly.

She helped me grow in many ways…in depth of love. She also connected me with other officers. Something not ordinarily done in the Army—enlisted men and officers together. So I experienced a different level of life and learning. Ideas—in many directions.

Keith told of visiting her family in Minneapolis after the war. Said he felt like he knew them, and they felt that way about him. He realized all the more why Karina was Karina. So Keith said he continues to stay in touch with her family—as he blinked away some tears.

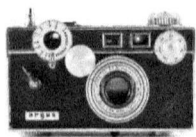

Review of Keith's presentation that night ranged from somber to elation.

Bob Felp, the *El Gaucho* editor, the history professor, the writer from the local paper, the photographers and even the publicist from the movie industry expressed how moved they felt as a result of the message. And they complimented Keith for his evocative presentation. They also agreed that the graphics support set a new high standard for such presentations.

Keith thanked all of them. Then he thanked me for roping him in, as he admitted he was wary of the task.

Then I felt embarrassed as he praised me for helping organize his thoughts, arranging for the graphics, and rehearsing the presentation with him.

Great teamwork! Great results! exclaimed the editor. And happy to have you on our newspaper staff, Sarah.

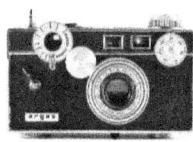

Chapter 11: Table-Hopping Surge

Everyone directly involved in the plan for the Table-Hopping Event spread the word among friends about the intent to bridge the interests of the younger students with a selected group of veterans in the college. Including some military women.

Keith led the way in recruiting interested and appropriate veterans and helped with the plan to deploy them at several tables.

He, like I, felt concern about how this idea might work. He also felt wary that such a gathering might get out of control, so he lined up volunteer MP's—Military Police—from his Army reserve unit to be on duty. Just in case.

But, appropriate to the situation, the experiment proceeded with military procession. Veterans moved into place, and the other students stopped by the tables for 10-minute discussions. We had intended to have the same students move on to other tables, but when we saw the large crowd of students eager to join in, we gave more a chance to drop in at a table.

I hadn't intended to participate in the table dialogue, but Keith insisted. So we went with two students to meet with four veterans at one table. Keith didn't know them, nor did I. But by this time, these veterans were adept at the discussion process, so we got acquainted quickly.

Then one young woman student posed a challenging question: will the proposed United Nations concept prevent more war?

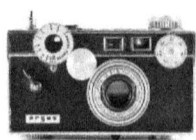

One veteran piped up. I think I can speak for my buddies to say that we hope so and count on it. But the tension in Europe and Asia remains high. So I say a definite maybe, he laughed.

BACKGROUND BRIEFING

The United Nations was conceived in October of 1945 at a conference in San Francisco, with a plan for a permanent headquarters in New York City. It aimed for international co-operation, replacing the earlier and ineffective League of Nations. At the start, the United Nations included 51 member countries.

Then other opinions surfaced. Keith interrupted to suggest this important issue deserves lots more attention, perhaps at other types of forums. Then he asked the woman who had raised the question if she would be willing to be part of a team to plan such a forum. She said yes, and one other young student and two veterans offered to help.

As the formal table-hopping concluded, a significant number of those involved continued to talk in mixed groups as they sampled the refreshments. Many sat again at the tables to expand on earlier dialogue. Even the MPs, sensing that their policing was not needed, shared in the refreshments and the discussions.

Bob Felp caught up with Keith and me to commend us for the successful experiment. We reminded him of the efficient and effective committee. He affirmed that and said the *El Gaucho* would credit all the leaders, plus featuring comments from them in the next issue. Also a sampling of reactions from those in the discussions.

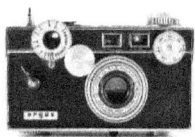

Sorry you didn't have time to take photos, Sarah. But you were rather busy. Another time.

Probably just as well I didn't plan to employ my humble Argus. With the excitement of the evening, good chance I would have managed more than one double-exposure. But, who knows what kind of intriguing crowd shot that might have produced.

That's a wrap, said another committee member, as she laughed about the Hollywood jargon.

We said good night as we went our separate ways. Me with my roommates and Keith with his fellow reservists.

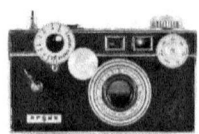

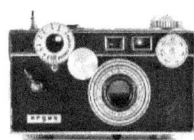

Chapter 12: Unusual Venue

After our next English class, Keith offered to me an invitation for the committee involved in the Table-Hopping project.

He mentioned that Bob intends to bring the group together for an evaluation of the experiment. Those of us reservists participating would like to invite your committee to meet over dinner at our improvised quarters.

That sounds…different, I responded. I can pass your invitation along to Bob, who could share it with the others. Then let you know.

Actually, I added, the idea sounds intriguing. Another way to bridge our differences. We could get better acquainted with you and the other reservists and thank all of you for your parts in the successful event.

Keith expanded on his invitation. You might find our improvised living quarters to be interesting, he said. We live in a small Quonset, next to the bigger Quonset for our military vehicles.

Let me sweeten the pot a little more, said Keith. You can count on a healthy and tasty dinner. Two of our unit had been cooks in the Army. But I'd call them chefs, because they learned a lot in the Army. Both have now started on a degree in food management and have already embarked on a project due for completion this fall.

Two others, said Keith as he added more incentive, intend to get a degree in agricultural engineering. Already they have volunteered to build a link with local farmers. As a byproduct, they get top quality vegetables and fruit for our meal preparation.

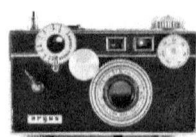

We also benefit from our military allotment for meat, milk, bread and other products. Of course, he added, we do have a well-appointed kitchen of Army surplus equipment and supplies.

In this weather, we could eat out on our patio, he chuckled.

Well, I said, your offer of a home-cooked meal sounds mighty appealing. I'm sure I can get an enthusiastic yes.

I'll report back immediately, sir, I said with a laugh shared by Keith.

In our dorm, I thought of the wartime slogan that loose lips sink ships. Rumors seem to be flying about the Table-Hopping Event, with strong hints that we should try that again so more could participate.

What a great way to meet men, they seem to imply—not particularly subtly either.

Still, not a bad idea, I thought. Might even be easier to arrange the next time.

The Table-Hopping Event caused what appeared to be a side effect for me. Several males had earlier shown interest in me and I in them. Now they evidently concluded that I belonged with Keith—a war veteran not to cross paths with. Reminds me of high school when other boys didn't ask me out because they thought I belonged to Stan the Con Man.

One of my friends mentioned that I must feel privileged to have an honor guard to watch out for me. Evidently the rumor mill had identified the MPs from the Table-Hopping as my personal guard.

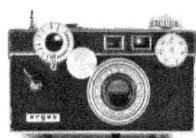

At least that creates a sense of security for me when I return to my dorm by myself after night meetings and classes.

Meanwhile, after I had passed along Keith's invitation, Bob and the others on the committee not only welcomed the invitation, but were studying their schedules to determine when they might take Keith up on his offer of dinner.

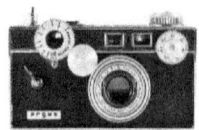

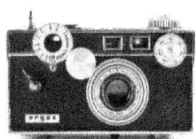

Chapter 13: Home-Front Speculation

A note from cousin Janet at Humboldt State included her phone number, so I decided to call rather than write.

After several rings, someone in her dorm answered. She shouted to Janet that she was wanted on the phone.

Janet was surprised and pleased to hear from me, and relieved that I was not the bearer of bad news.

Just a chat, I said.

I apologized for not writing recently, but explained how busy I've been. At her prompting, I summarized what I'm involved in.

When she asked about my love life, I explained the complication. I got acquainted with an Army veteran who sits next to me in our English class. Because some others in the class from our dorm had seen Keith and me talking, they now call him my good-looking man-friend—because he's a mature veteran here on the G.I. Bill.

Well, actually, he's only 21, but he seems much more mature.

I explained that I and several others from the student newspaper staff had helped Keith make a presentation at a history class about his wartime experience.

No, I wouldn't call him cute, I answered Janet's question. Handsome would be more appropriate. We're getting acquainted because we are both part of plan to create a bridge between the younger students and the veterans.

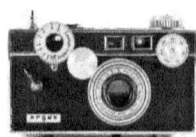

Well, actually, I initiated a project called Table-Hopping, I explained in response to Janet's surprise. We had a great initial event and hope to socialize more this way.

Then I distracted her by asking about her love life. She admitted that she too got acquainted with a veteran who seems much more interesting than the shallow conventional students.

Welcome to the club! I declared.

Timely reminder, I answered, when she told me she had seen my family on a recent visit home. Yes, I will give them a call to satisfy their curiosity—or concern—about my college life.

With that, we rang off, with promises to stay in touch. By mail and phone.

But next I phoned home.

When Mom answered, she asked Dad to take the other line, and I repeated what I had told Janet.

Great to hear your voice and hear about your interesting activities, said Mom, after I described my busy and interesting life.

After I told of my acquaintance with Keith and my description of him, Dad happily responded with the thought that your mature friend is helping you mature quickly.

Hadn't thought that much about it, I admitted. But you're right, Dad.

Before you ask, I added, my other classes chug along steadily. I think I will do fine.

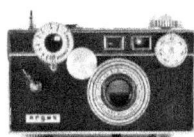

By the way, I'm using my Argus as part of my work for the student newspaper. Others envy the C3, and I've learned to be patient and careful with it.

As to social life, you wouldn't believe what's coming up. Keith and his Army reserve friends have invited our event team to have dinner with them at their Army reserve quarters. Then we will evaluate our Table-Hopping project.

Keith assures us that his team has great culinary skills. We'll soon see. And I'll let you know.

Naturally, Mom and Dad were curious about my relationship with Keith.

No, he's not my boyfriend—or man-friend as my roommates say. For one thing, he's still in love with his nurse Karina, who was killed during the Battle of the Bulge. Don't know what I'd want, or what to expect with him.

After their brief updates about home, we mutually agreed to a series of regular phone exchanges.

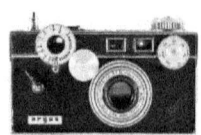

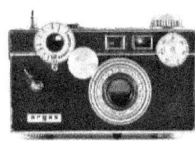

Chapter 14: Army Chow

Right on schedule, Keith drove up in his military troop truck to our meeting place in front of the student center.

He and another sergeant hopped out of the truck to help eight of us into the back of the truck. The sergeant explained that at least the seats were padded. More than what the GIs got in combat.

He stopped me and said I should climb into the cab with Keith, while he sat with the others of our groups to answer questions or share information. He informed me and the others that we only had to travel a few miles to the Veterans Village, and the route is not bumpy.

With the tailgate up in place and me in the front passenger seat, Keith started to climb in.

Then one in a line of puzzled students shouted, Can we come too?

Keith saluted casually and smiled and said, Sorry, top secret maneuver.

He saluted again when we entered the Village and a guard smiled and waved us through.

When we pulled up in front a huge Quonset building, more veterans met us and helped me and the others down.

I asked, aren't you the MPs at our meeting? They nodded yes and laughed as they welcomed us.

Then we walked to a patio in front of the smaller Quonset, where steaks sizzled on an improvised barbeque unit tended by the Chefs.

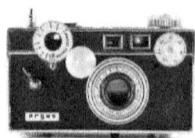

Decorated cloths covered the banquet table, which was set with napkins, plates, tableware, and glasses and cups.

Our group waited in awe as Keith urged us to sit at random, with the veteran students mixed in. Like our Table-Hopping event. Then Keith offered a prayer of thankfulness about the end of the war, about the opportunity for education, for interesting friends…and for delicious chow.

Then the reservist waiters checked with each for preference about steaks, and soon they brought the rare steaks, followed by medium and then well done.

Keith laughed that the food carts were usually loaded with tools, so they should be sturdy enough for this duty too.

The chief waiter, who was studying food management, announced that the vegetable salad was farm fresh and the bread had been baked in the food class at the college. He offered choices of drinks: cold spring water, various juices concocted in the food class, and coffee or tea specially blended in the class.

Besides sharing from the ample and tasty food, the members of our group shared thoughts about the mixture of students now affecting many campuses. Soon we had also developed a feeling of camaraderie in this mixed group. That led naturally into a review of our Table-Hopping project. The consensus: Great start, great growth in mutual understanding, and great hope for such events in the future.

Then, as most sipped coffee to conclude the event, the head Chef and assistants rolled carts to the tables with a special dessert. He explained that a merengue covers ice cream as it is baked. Called Baked Alaska, it relates to the cold of Scandinavia, so tonight it

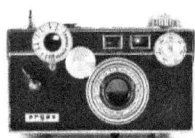

honors two of Scandinavian descent, Sarah Karlstrom and Keith Kragstad.

The ooh's and aah's continued as the guests tasted the special dessert.

BACKGROUND BRIEFING

Despite jokes about attempts to pound square pegs into round holes, the American military forces effectively trained a vast array of men and women during World War II. Some programs emphasized repetitive tasks, while other options included study of many subjects at a variety of colleges and universities. West Point, Annapolis and other military schools stressed development of military leadership.

The guests thanked the Chef and Keith. A masterful ending of a marvelous meal, pronounced Bob, as the others cheered and clapped.

Before all of us boarded the troop-truck again, Keith invited us to take a quick look at both Quonsets. In the smaller building, we saw the neatly arranged bedroom cubicles and the shared kitchen and dining area. A pool table served also as a support for a Ping Pong table, which in turn, Keith explained, serves as a work table to lay out vehicle instruction sheets and blueprints of construction projects.

The bigger building provided a bigger surprise. In the middle of a room, surrounded by an array of tools and parts, a hydraulic lift raised a bright-colored Hot Rod. Like a piece of sculpture.

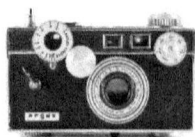

I impressed Keith when I said I knew what it is. And I told him about my high school classmate who is building and writing about his Hot Rod. When I mentioned that I had heard that a new Hot Rod magazine is on the horizon to be published in our area, he admitted that he hopes he might interest the publication in reporting about the Army-reserve Hot Rod.

Good chance for me to take some photos, with the Hot Rod up on the lift, then down.

First I took some straight shots. Then I decided to test the Argus C3 by intentionally taking advantage of its weakness—double exposure. I needed my tripod to be sure the camera stayed in place. And steady. For one shot, I asked Keith to be at a position in front of the Hot Rod. Then I suggested he position himself with the engine visible. Next, the third exposure showed him at the driver's door.

I aimed, literally, to put him in different parts of the printed photo. The light seemed cooperative, so I crossed my fingers and hoped for the best.

The bulletin board caught the eye of Bob Felp, and he called out attention to a drawing by the military cartoonist Bill Mauldin. Keith explained that he's a favorite artist among the enlisted men, and Mauldin often got in trouble with the brass for his jibes about officers.

We cherish this one, explained Keith, as he pointed out the soldier from a cavalry unit ready to fire his pistol at his crippled Jeep.

For our newspaper bunch, that led to a discussion of the word Jeep. We heard many stories about the name, explained Keith, but I understand that it came from guys like us, who named it for Eugene the Jeep in the comic strip *Popeye*.

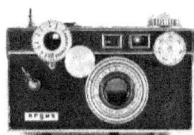

Like our Jeep, that Jeep was small and adaptable for dealing with impossible challenges.

Here's another bit of war history, said Keith. See that drawing of a man looking over a wall, clinging by his hands with nose and eyes just above the wall.

That's the ubiquitous Kilroy, who seemed to appear everywhere in the war. *Kilroy was here!* had become a slogan of surprise to serve as another bit of humor to boost spirits.

As we climbed into our chariot, Bob called our evening remarkable. Let's keep this process going, he added.

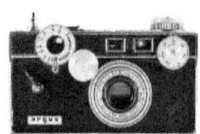

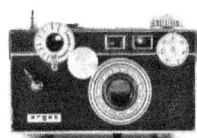

Chapter 15: What do I want to be?

Good question, I admitted, when Bob asked if I knew what I want to be. You seem interested in and show potential for journalism, he said.

Journalism offers great training and experience in writing and graphics, including photography, he stressed. Your writing and speaking would fit working for the campus radio station too. You know how to show off your good looks, and Hollywood needs your talents and skills as well as beauty. And the same for the boom in television.

Now you're laying it on thick, I laughed. But you're right about my interests and aptitudes, I conceded. I lean more toward socializing than science.

I thought so, said Bob, the way you organized and facilitated our Table-Hopping Event. And the follow-up.

What do you think, folks? he asked others of the group in the newspaper staff meeting. Can we help Sarah map out her matriculation?

The others responded: You bet! Sure can! Make you a student leader. Got you pegged for student senate. Your success might help us too.

Good that you're signed up for the basics for now, said Bob. Later, what?

Psychology, said one. Political science, said another. Others tossed in physical sciences, advanced math, Spanish for our area.

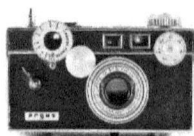

Guess that would put you on track to be a student leader, said Bob.

Better add chemistry and art, I laughed, or my parents will be disappointed.

Then for starters in art, said Bob, I would like to have you photograph and write about an unusual expression of contemporary art—the Hot Rod that Keith and his Motor Pool team are building.

The design of the Hot Rod and the graphics on it fit a trend notable in Southern California. That would also continue our emphasis on bridging the younger students with the veterans.

Oh yes, I replied, I noticed and admired the colors of their Hot Rod. Dramatic flair with a tie to the Army. The yellow and teal V stripes on the mottled green of the roadster body look unique and very contemporary. I took several photos, including a triple exposure as an experiment. I'll let you know how that turns out.

Sounds like a good theme for the story. And another good link for you with Keith, said Bob, with a grin.

Maybe you could turn that into a story for the Hot Rod magazine while you're at it, he suggested.

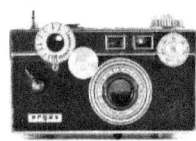

Chapter 16: Side Car becomes a Sidebar

Guess we'll have to get crackin', laughed Keith when I told him of our hope to publicize his Hot Rod.

Our Hot Rod, he corrected me. We're a regular pit crew, working on this project together. And I'm sure the others will welcome some attention, instead of just me.

As you saw, Keith explained, we've nearly finished the outside of our Rod, but now we're goosing the engine. That Model B Ford will put out a lot more power than it ever experienced before. I'll let you know when we can take a spin.

But how about another type of spin—on my motorcycle? Ever ride one? he asked.

Nope, too scary for me, I admitted, as I told him more about the car accident that killed my classmate.

Then I mentioned how scared I during a short ride in that convertible with Stan the Con Man. When he stepped on the gas to show off, the whole car started shaking. And so did I.

Called shimmying, explained Keith, from problems with the steering. Tires not balanced and aligned, or a fault with the steering mechanism. Strange, with that usually-dependable Cadillac.

Well, I'll attach the side-car for safety and comfort. A little comfort, anyway. We can make a dramatic departure after our next English class for a cruise to the Motor Pool, so you can learn more about our Hot Rod and some of the others working on it.

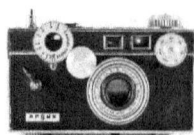

You'll impress gawkers on campus as they see you whisked away in my chariot, he grinned. You'll be like Cinderella when your campus friends see you climbing into that Army-green side car. Better wear slacks though so you can scrunch into tight space. And to keep warm.

I laughed to myself when I thought about the situation. And my side-car experience could make a good sidebar to our main story of the Hot Rod. Or a preview of the story to come. Better have my Argus along to record my side-car experience. Draft a volunteer to snap shots of me in the group.

At the Motor Pool, he said he was still pondering the mystery of the shaking Cadillac. After the other mechanics welcomed me back, Keith told them about the '41 Cadillac convertible going out of control and flipping over.

Sorry about your classmate, he said to me, but I sure am thankful it wasn't you.

He wondered why it flipped over. Need your help with that puzzle, he said to the others.

A simple possibility, offered one. If lover-boy focused on his girl-friend and not on the road, he could have veered off the edge of the pavement. A sudden correction could have put the car out of control.

But he claims he wasn't with Stacy Moore, I said. So no one knows what happened.

Strange about the shimmy, said another. Seems like the owner of such an expensive car would have kept it good condition. Maybe damaged connecting rods for the steering weren't repaired properly.

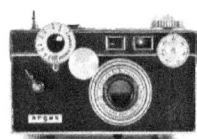

Let me know if you come up with any other reasons, said Keith. Now we have to show off our Hot Rod. Sarah plans to write about it for the college newspaper. Maybe even try to interest a new Hot Rod magazine in a story, too.

How about some fresh coffee and a cinnamon roll first, suggested the mechanic also known as the Chef. We can tell over coffee about the why we decided to build this torpedo and what it is.

BACKGROUND BRIEFING

Hot Rods blossomed in the late 1930s in Southern California (maybe sired earlier by fleeing Bootleggers during Prohibition). The activity increased in popularity after World War II, because many returning soldiers had been given technical training. They especially reworked Ford Model T's, A's and B's for top performance. Then they jazzed up their Hot Rods with fancy graphics too. Some army artists checked with sign companies about how they created large billboards. So they learned to create and fasten paper templates with holes cut to outline designs. Using a pounce pad, they marked the design through the holes onto the Hot Rod. That became the guide for the painted design.

As we sipped our coffee and indulged in a cinnamon roll, he explained that after the war the Army wanted to get rid of a lot of soldiers but hang on to some with special skills. So the Army indulges us reservists—actually encourages us—to experiment in ways such as our Hot Rod.

Good to have access to Army resources and tools, of course.

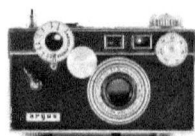

Keith here, for example, learned about hydraulics as a teenager in his family's garage. Like our hydraulic lift for our vehicles. So we've added hydraulic brakes and other controls. Hydraulics also power some of our tools, for instance. And air pressure works in a similar way.

Both types of power provide the action for what we call our Clown-mobiles, because the bodies of the vehicles move up and down and in a supposedly random way. So do the clowns. Hope to offer them to perform at local celebrations.

The Army PIO—Public Information Office—wants to show off the Clown-mobile and our new Hot Rod. Get publicity for the Army.

Even enter both in the January Rose Parade in Pasadena.

Another mechanic provided show-and-tell about the Hot Rod, pointing out some of the special features. He explained that his own Ford came with a V-8 engine, but not with the power of this one. We souped-up this one with turbo-assist and fuel injection.

Maybe someday, said Keith, we'll add some rockets to send this shooting off the starting blocks. Then the Batmobile would have nothing on us!

I understood some of the show-and-tell, and at least acted interested even when I didn't soak up the details. But I did get a feel for the knowledge and enthusiasm of these student-veterans. And got a sense what they might accomplish in the future.

That would be the heart of the story I'd write, to accompany a variety of photos I took with my Argus.

Maybe with the triple-exposure if that turns out the way I hope it might.

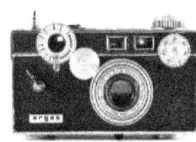

Chapter 17: Putting the Pieces Together

While I struggled to cobble-together a feature story tying the Motor Pool to the college, Keith said his team was trying to figure out the wreck of the Cadillac.

When he asked whether I had a photo of the car, I said I had kept one that shows my friend in the driver's seat. I had printed it from one of my usable negatives, not the double-exposures, as I frowned with a bit of embarrassment about my mistake.

Maybe it reminded me of my feeling of guilt from introducing Stacy to Stan the Con Man.

Great! said Keith when I showed him my photo. This even shows the license number, he exclaimed. So maybe we can track down the car in a wrecking yard up north. Some other Army reservists go to school up there, so we'll ask for a helping hand.

I needed a helping hand with my story, too. Bob and others on the news staff liked my first draft, but had some suggestions to intensify the relationship of the veterans to the college.

Back to the drawing board for me, after some helpful evaluation.

Great stuff! Bob said about my photos from the Motor Pool. Your extra lenses sure proved their value. Your wide-angles and close-ups provide a welcome range of selections, he said. And your triple-exposure is a *tour de force*. Almost like a movie.

By the way, he added, we have some glamorous shots of you climbing into the side car. We like the old aircraft helmet and goggles on Keith too. Those will be great teasers for your story.

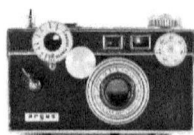

After the next English class, I showed Keith some of my photos. And I mentioned that the draft of my story about his team still needed some polishing. But I warned him that the side-car photos would be in the *El Gaucho* in the near future—to promote the coming larger story.

This I really like, he declared, as he studied the triple-exposure. I'm a one-man band, he laughed.

In his usual under-stated manner, he then smiled warmly at me to express his appreciation.

Then Keith provided his progress report about the investigation of Stan's Cadillac.

May take some time, he explained, but we've expanded our investigative reach. Maybe we'll eventually get a chance to check out the Cadillac ourselves.

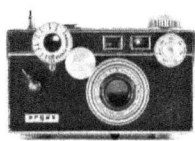

Chapter 18: Fall Break

Despite my growing and interesting involvement at college, I welcomed the Thanksgiving break to be with my family and friends. And to savor our traditional dinner.

Keith volunteered to take me to the train station, this time in a Jeep. The side car, he declared with a grin, wouldn't hold my luggage. And the Hot Rod, he had laughed, wasn't quite ready for street use. Or any use, yet.

BACKGROUND BRIEFING

What's in a name? The ubiquitous all-purpose Jeep evidently first got its name from a government designation, but soldiers and sailors picked their own name for the popular vehicle from the comic strip *Popeye*. Willys first and then Ford cranked out thousands of the adaptable Jeeps for all branches of the services. Later, the Jeep was modified for a variety of civilian uses, including the varied needs of farmers and ranchers.

Hope you have a relaxing time, he said. We'll miss you…but you'll miss our Thanksgiving feast at the Motor Pool.

We even plan to test some wine that's part of a college agriculture program our Chefs participate in. Seems like a market with potential. Still, he said, if you'll pardon bar tending, you're too young to drink anyway. But we'll toast you with thanks for how you're supporting us veterans in college.

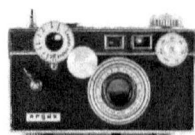

When I got off the train at the small station near our home, I looked for our big black Buick. Ought to be easy to spot, I thought.

Then I saw Mom and Dad heading my way, with big smiles and open arms.

After emotional hugs, they declared "welcome home!"

Dad grabbed my suitcase and we headed for the parking lot. I still didn't see the Buick. Then they stopped by a small black car that looked like a reduced-size '41 Ford sedan.

We drove this instead of the Buick, said Dad. Our new second car. It's much smaller for getting around town. Better gas mileage too!

What is it? I asked.

A new Volvo from Sweden, said Dad. A PV61, to be precise.

Our Swedish friend from church now sells Volvos, said Mom. Dad heard of the high quality of Volvos, and our friend confirmed it. Also, because our friend's an official dealer, we can count on dependable service.

Dad laughed when I asked if the steering wheel is on the left.

Yup, Americanized, so it is different from the same car in Sweden.

Dad put my suitcase in the trunk, and I climbed into the back seat. Cozy, I said, when I actually meant tiny. But comfortable, I added, as I settled in.

Well, finally I said, after I repeated the great surprise about the Volvo, you two still look great! I'm mighty happy to be back with

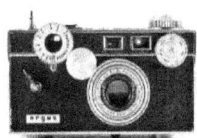

you! And I'm waiting for the other shoe to drop, if you have more surprises.

Only the Volvo, said Mom. But you've written about several of your surprises, so we're eager to hear more. But you can relax now, and tell about your new life to all of us during our Thanksgiving dinner.

I'll at least tell you about my surprising "taxi." I went to the train station in Santa Barbara in an Army Jeep, which is at the disposal of my Army reservist friend Keith. Before that I rode in the side-car of his motorcycle. That should whet your appetite for more…later.

As the Volvo pulled up to our house, a midget next to the Buick, I felt new appreciation for the beauty of our home.

Don't know if I ever wondered before, I said, but how did you find and afford this place?

Well, we were struck by its simple and natural beauty. Designed by an architect named Bernard Maybeck, and most of his structures use shingles, rough redwood interiors, and huge hand-wrought fireplaces. He taught for a time at Cal in Berkeley and designed a variety of building there—in his style, of course.

Isn't this neighborhood a bit pricey, Dad?

Now, but not when we bought this house in 1941. Maybeck's style hadn't caught on yet at that time.

So we got a bargain, said Mom. Even at that, we had to skimp to afford it. The closeness of the railway station added to its appeal.

Glad you got it, I concurred. A real treasure. I recall how we loved this place and our neighborhood.

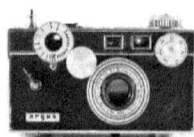

Now, to whet your appetite for tomorrow, said Mom, we will offer the usual grand Thanksgiving dinner. And your help will be much appreciated.

Usual and grand, that's what I'm counting on, I said. And I'll be glad to assist, while I learn from the master—or mistress.

Later in the evening, Dad asked about my interest in chemistry.

Still there, but your influence in photography continues, too, so I'm leaning toward journalism. Altered my focus, so to speak, I laughed.

Anyway, my involvement in the student newspaper has also motivated me to a more-disciplined approach to my classes.

In my art class, Mom, my photography earned praise for the composition and varied exposures. With my Argus, I even produced a triple-exposure that led to compliments—and discussion in the class.

And I demonstrated the alternatives enabled by the three lenses.

And here's the triple-exposed photo as it appeared in the *El Gaucho,* our student newspaper. And it features Keith and his evolving Hot Rod.

Great work! complemented Dad, as he studied the photo in the newspaper.

Then Mom postulated: You've written quite a bit about Keith. Love life?

Good friend. But he hugged me once in an unusual expression of enthusiasm from him.

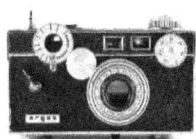

That certainly felt special for me, considering his usual Scandinavian Stoicism.

Anyway, I assured Mom, I'll tell all during dinner tomorrow. Then you can judge our friendship.

Whatever our relationship, I cherish it.

BACKGROUND BRIEFING

In describing Keith, Sarah said that he fits her perception of Scandinavians. Friendly, kind, cautious and somewhat reserved. Punctual and efficient. They believe in giving individuals freedom, opportunity and responsibility. And participation in decisions. Like our family. Well, most of the time anyway.

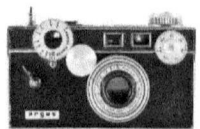

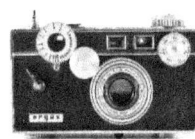

Chapter 19: Dinner Dialogue

Cousin Janet and her parents, Dad's brother Paul and his wife Emily, came from nearby Mountain View to join in our holiday celebration.

Soon after that, brother Bill arrived—with a lovely Stanford coed.

Meet Carla Mason, he announced as we chatted before the meal.

Then Janet and I and Carla went to work helping Mom with the fixings for Thanksgiving. All the usual traditional and delicious stuff, including stuffing.

I thought of Keith and his cohorts preparing their unusual meal, according to the menu he had described. The wine there would be a mystery selected by the Chefs of the Motor Pool, obtained directly from a vineyard that is part of their study of regional agriculture.

Keith had chuckled in explaining that he would not have poured any for me. Too young, he said. Like a protective older brother.

At dinner, I laughed as brother Bill poured wine for me as well, and then he wondered about the humor of it. I told him about the rules set by Keith, in which I would have to abstain from the wines selected by the Chefs in the agricultural studies program at Cal Poly. Too young by a year.

After a thoughtful prayer of thanks by Dad, we focused on food.

As we progressed in our feast, Mom asked again about Keith.

Tell more, said Bill, as Carla and Janet looked particularly curious.

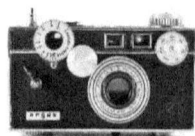

It's complicated, I started. As you can probably guess by the post-war change in college education, Santa Barbara has had a surge of veterans attending as part of the G.I. Bill of Rights.

Great boon to education, said Dad, as the others nodded in agreement.

Yeah, said Janet, the veterans make up almost half of the student body at Humboldt State. They seem like a great bunch, though we haven't had much chance to get acquainted with each other on campus. A lot of them are married, so they probably wouldn't participate much in student activities anyway.

That brings me back to Keith, I explained, who is an Army veteran. And he is in the active Army reserve, which means he's on duty some of the time. I got acquainted with him because of the alphabet, I laughed.

That sounds intriguing, said Carla. Continue, please.

His name is Kragstad, so he sits alphabetically next to me.

Laughing about our Scandinavian names broke the ice in talking with this reserved veteran—if you'll pardon the link to his being in the active reserve.

Oh no! laughed Bill. But I'll reserve judgment.

I think this might be a loving matter, not a laughing matter, interjected Mom, considering how much we've heard about Keith.

Well, back to what we were discussing—about getting acquainted with veterans. I shared with our dorm leaders about how we might bridge the association of the younger students with the veterans.

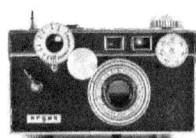

Then the student government asked me to get involved. At the same time the student newspaper got interested, and I got interested in the student newspaper. So I suggested a Table-Hopping social event as a way for veterans to meet other students. And vice versa. So I enlisted Keith's help in reaching the veterans. And he and I gradually became good friends.

Sounds like a love match to me, said Janet. You told me that Keith is tall and good looking.

Well, yes, I continued, a bit flustered.

Anyway, he subsequently became a spokesman for the veterans when he was asked by a history professor to share a veteran's response about the war.

I helped him with a presentation plan and enlisted the aid of the student newspaper photographers. They even connected with Hollywood movie sources for graphics.

As a result, his show about the Battle of the Bulge proved to be a great hit, attracting an audience much broader than just the history class.

So, I admit admiration. If this is love, Mom, it is slow blooming. But as I said, Keith did hug me once.

That's a start, said Mom.

Well, I have been accepted into an unusual fraternity, I explained.

A fraternity? inquired Bill. Not a sorority as you had visualized?

A radical change. Unofficial, I said. This fraternity is the Motor Pool. Operated by the Army reserve.

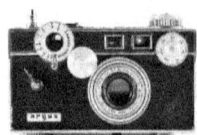

So that's why you rode in the motorcycle side car, laughed Dad. Wouldn't mind trying that myself.

Me too! exclaimed Janet.

Squeeze me in also, chuckled Carla.

That makes a good segue to you, Carla. Where are you from? And how did you meet Bill our football hero?

I'm from Wisconsin, she said. This will help you remember—I'm Mason from Madison. Both my parents teach at the University of Wisconsin. But I wanted to spread my wings and go West. And escape the cold weather in Wisconsin, she chuckled.

So Stanford took me in.

Not so many veterans there, so I found this tall and handsome football player, she smiled as she put her hand on his arm.

Yeah, linking with Carla is one the best moves in my football career, laughed Bill.

Your turn, Janet, to confess, I said.

Humboldt State is called the Lumberjacks, she said, and I found one in my beginning forestry class. He's a veteran also, because we've got lots of them. Lars is from the north woods of Minnesota, where his family owns a logging and lumber operation.

Tall, blond and handsome—and Swedish.

That's a winning combination, said Dad.

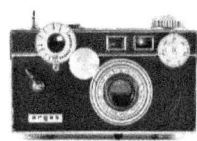

Chapter 20: Motor-Pool Musings

Everyone seemed puzzled and inquisitive about our Motor Pool.

First, I explained that the main purpose of a working Motor Pool is to supply and service all kinds of vehicles operated out of the regular Army unit between here and Santa Barbara.

I told about Keith leading a special Army research project using a large Quonset building for storage and another smaller one for housing. They squeeze those into a special site in the military airport in Goleto, near Santa Barbara.

He aims to be an engineer, so he and others are experimenting, particularly with hydraulics and electronics.

Nutrition also gets attention from the Army, so the Chefs in his unit are students as part of the agricultural emphasis at the college. They also coordinate with Cal Poly at San Luis Obispo. Let me tell you, these Chefs put out some good food!

The Motor Pool team offered an appealing surprise at one home football game.

Keith had cordoned off a couple of parking spaces near the stadium and had invited me and the gang from the student newspaper and radio staffs to meet there. Keith even had his MPs on guard there to protect the territory.

Then the Motor Pool troop truck rolled in. The Chefs dropped the tailgate, set out a serving table, and loaded it with healthful fruit bars and fruit juices.

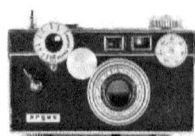

To the envy of other fans, we stood around talking and munching before the start of the game. Which we won, by the way. Sports reporters there to cover the game took time to report about our picnic too. So we shared some Motor Pool grub with them.

What a way to start a game, laughed Bill. But you may also have launched a trend.

Sorry, I said to Bill, that your Stanford team will not be in the Rose Bowl. Even though your team record is 6-3-1. Our Gauchos compiled a pretty good record too.

Apples and oranges, said Bill. We play a much tougher schedule, as you know.

By the way, he added, I was thrilled recently to meet Stanford's star alum, All-American Frankie Albert.

Great to have him playing for the San Francisco 49ers. A new team and the first professional team on the West Coast.

Wouldn't mind meeting him myself, I stated.

And I do recognize the difference in the caliber of college competition, I admitted. Hope Stanford makes it into the Rose Bowl next year.

And I hope our Motor Pool Hot Rod makes it to the next Rose Parade too. The Army hopes to get good public relations that way.

Certainly appropriate for Los Angeles, the car capital of the world.

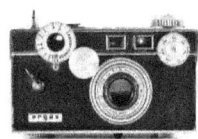

Well, Christine, I guess we should plan to take in the Rose Bowl, said Dad. At least the parade, he smiled. Maybe we could make it a family affair, he added, as he looked to the others.

BACKGROUND BRIEFING

As one of the largest cities in the world, Los Angeles (Spanish for City of Angels) also has one of the greatest mixtures of people, places and activities. It promotes all types of art, and businesses range from the noted movie industry to broadcasting, oil production and many dimensions of aerospace. Though LA borders the Pacific Ocean, aqueducts bring potable water.

What's so special about your Hot Rod? Bill then asked.

Here's what I can remember, I explained. It grew from a Model B Ford, so it has provision for a huge V-8 engine. Turbo-charged besides. Fuel injection, whatever that means. And radical new multi-speed transmission.

The Motor Pool buildings nestle in a corner of the huge military air base, so Keith and the others get the latest on aircraft improvements, such as fuel injection. What next? Maybe rocket propulsion, I laughed.

Remember, Janet, when we would ride our bikes to try to get as close as possible to Moffett Field to see every kind of aircraft we could imagine? Not far from you in Mountain View.

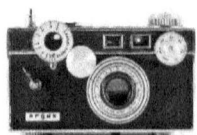

Yeah, we saw planes every day during the war, but those massive balloons made the biggest impression on us, answered Janet.

I remember that huge hanger there, said Bill. Great bonus to watch the action when we went to your place in the summer—like on the Fourth of July.

Of course, your root beer floats left a fond memory too. And I learned a lot just listening to Dad and your dad talk about the war. Great way to honor Independence Day.

Well, in our small Quonset Hut, our Hot Rod dazzles with its gold stripes—maybe sergeant's stripes—over a glistening medium green.

Listen to that possessiveness, laughed Bill. *Our* Hot Rod in *our* Quonset!

Seems that way sometimes, I answered. Anyway, I smiled, I've already drafted an article about *our* Hot Rod for the college newspaper and have taken a collection of photos.

You'll be proud, Dad, that I'm putting my Argus C3 to good use.

We hope a new Hot Rod magazine being planned in Los Angeles will be interested in a story about *our* Hot Rod too.

By the way, Dad, to change the subject to another type of car—your new Volvo purrs like a kitten.

How'd that come about, Dad? asked Bill.

Volvo just started selling cars in the United States, and our friend Hans recommended it. He sells and services them. They're known for quality, efficiency and safety. So we're Swedish pioneers, you might say.

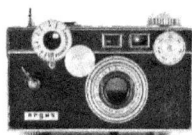

Chapter 21: Early Investigation

Janet and Bill, I asked, do you remember the auto accident that killed my high school classmate, Stacy Moore?

Oh yes, a real beauty queen, said Janet.

And her boyfriend—your passing acquaintance—was a conniving jerk, said Bill. Still is, I heard.

Somehow, Stacy's accident still haunts me, as I explained my reason for mentioning it. I had introduced her to Stan the Con Man.

Intriguing, said Carla. Makes me want to know more.

Emily and I have wondered about that tragic incident ever since Janet mentioned it, said Paul.

I still feel guilt from introducing Stacy to Stan the Con Man. Maybe I did it out of spite. Angry with him and jealous of her. Thought it would serve Miss Beauty Queen right.

Anyway, I never dreamed that it would create a tragic ending for her. Stan accepted no blame for Stacy being killed in his car. Out of town at the time, he said.

Well, at the time, said Bill, I had mentioned that the Logans— including Stan the Con Man—operated a shady Black Market business. I admit it has made them rich. And being rich seemed to make them respectable and trusted.

What's a Black Market business? Carla asked, as she sought to understand the situation.

Is it legal? she asked Bill.

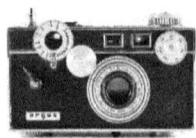

Depends, I guess, said Bill. Maybe I can learn more through our law professors if needed. Just buying low and selling high would be okay, but buying low and patching up cars and machinery just to look good and cover up problems certainly seems unlawful.

Caveat emptor, or buyer beware, prevails unless the seller conceals faults. That shifts to *caveat venditor,* in which the seller must be aware of responsibility. Profiteering also seems to fit the Logans, for taking excessive profits from essential goods during a time of emergency.

Murky at best.

Don't feel too much guilt, Sarah. Stacy should have been wary of Stan the Con Man. After all, lots of students at our school knew of his character.

I explained that even my friend Keith finds the accident questionable. He's puzzled about how a heavy Cadillac convertible could tip over, just by going off the edge of the paving. When I explained that Cadillac shook when Stan the Con Man drove it at higher speeds, Keith and the other mechanics at the Motor Pool

BACKGROUND BRIEFING

The sleek '41 Cadillac convertible featured many special design elements, such as rectangular parking lights built into the top outer corners of the grille, headlights in the nose of the fenders with built in accessory fog lights under the headlights. Rear fender skirts were standard. The Series 62 offered the only 4-door convertible built by Cadillac in 1941.

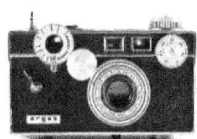

wondered about the condition of the steering mechanism in the front.

I shared a photo of Stacy in the Cadillac I took before the community parade, and that shows the license number. So Keith has asked for help from guys in a Motor Pool up here to try to find and check that car.

I hope it hasn't just been patched up again and sold to someone else.

Certainly a possibility, said Bill.

Sounds like greed combined with dishonesty, said Carla. All the others nodded to indicate they shared Carla's opinion.

Keep us posted, said Bill.

By the way, if I have time, I'll enlarge all of the photos I took the day of the parade. Even the double-exposures caused by my Argus C3. Stan the Con Man said that he was in Fresno scouting for farm equipment that day, but in the back of my mind I sense he was at the parade. He may show in one of those two double-exposed negatives.

At the time, I didn't even bother to make prints of them because I figured they had no value. But maybe Stan does show a bit in those double-exposures.

Do we still have those negatives, Dad?

Yup, not cut apart and still in a protective sleeve, hanging in the dark room—as a reminder, of course, he smiled.

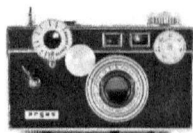

Could indicate he was lying about his whereabouts that day, said Bill. Could be enough to start an investigation.

Sounds like an Edgar Allen Poe mystery, said Janet. Or Sherlock Holmes, offered Carla. Or a negative solution, added Dad.

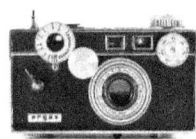

Chapter 22: Loose Ends of Love

I hope your current relationship with Keith, said Mom, turns out to be far better than your brief infatuation with Stan the Con Man, as you call him.

No comparison, I said. Keith's a talented, honorable person. Here's his picture in the student newspaper during his presentation about the Battle of the Bulge, I said, as I gave it to Mom to share with the others.

Good looking, all right, smiled Mom.

Keith's car knowledge, I explained, started in the garage and service station his family operates in a small town near Lincoln, Nebraska. His parents and a brother and sister still live in that area. He's a bit chauvinistic about Nebraska.

He urged me to read a novel by his favorite author from there, Willa Cather. Said she elevates the role of women in life today. He laughed when he predicted that Alexandra in *O Pioneers!* should certainly inspire me.

I remember that wonderful story, said Mom. Have you read it?

Yes, and it does inspire me. Cather was the first woman graduate of the University of Nebraska, and her character Alexandra comes across as a creative and determined woman managing a farm.

Keith's story is inspirational as well.

In an unusual way, his military service motivated him to attend college. Maybe love encouraged him too.

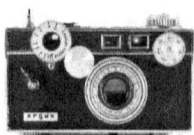

One of his assignments included driving an ambulance during battles. Through that dangerous work, he became acquainted with a nurse named Karina Johanson.

As an officer, she arranged for him to move beyond the traditional military separation of officers from enlisted men. And through friendship with her and the other officers, he began to see the value of higher education.

When the Motor Pool hosted our newspaper staff to a gourmet lunch, Keith showed me a cartoon posted on the bulletin board. By Army cartoonist Bill Mauldin as he satirized the hierarchy. This cartoon shows two officers looking at a mountain vista. One officer asks the other if there's also a view for enlisted men.

Yeah, said Dad, Mauldin drew biting cartoons about the military brass. When some officers complained to General Eisenhower, he dismissed their protests, saying such humor boosted morale among the troops.

Keith also said, I added, that he and Karina violated another military rule of separation, as they became romantically involved. Even planned to get married after the war. But during the terrible Battle of the Bulge, when they were tending the wounded, a German mortar hit right where she was helping an injured soldier. She and the soldier both died instantly.

I think Keith died emotionally for a time. He has visited and become friends with Karina's family in Minneapolis, but I think she continues as an empty part of his life.

So I'm just glad he is my friend—though I might like him to be more than that.

Well, he did hug you once, laughed Mom, with a tear in her eye.

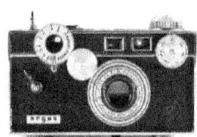

A good start, said a misty Carla.

You're moving up, Janet said softly.

I sensed that the men of the family affirmed quietly, without comment.

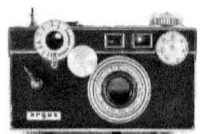

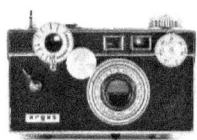

Chapter 23: Return to the Campus

I was thankful for the enjoyable and restful Thanksgiving break, but I also looked forward to being back on campus.

My first weeks at Santa Barbara had proven to be stimulating, far more than I could have guessed. Partly luck, but my own talent and temperament for making the best of opportunity began to emerge.

I also looked forward to being back with many other students, especially those who were not only my friends but who engaged me in interesting and rewarding activities.

I realized that I particularly counted on being with Keith and his Motor Pool associates. What a unique bunch! Serious but enjoying life in creative ways. Admired by a variety of many others.

Little wonder that at the train station they brightened my return. Not the side car or the Jeep this time, but the troop truck with the Motor Pool bunch to welcome me back. I looked around to be sure they weren't here for some other reason. If my tears showed, I didn't care, I was so honored.

Keith grabbed my suitcase in one hand and my hand in the other as he helped me off the train. Meanwhile, the Chefs had set out their usually tasty fruit bars and juice, as one of the MPs offered a soft trumpet welcome.

With that, we were all smiles. And so were many others getting off or boarding the train. Or were on the platform for arriving and departing friends and relatives.

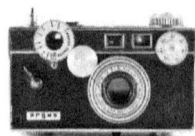

Then I realized the group included some coeds. Editor Bob laughed when he noted my surprise. Seems that writing and oil do mix, he explained with a chuckle, because some special friendships have evolved as a result of the journalism coverage of the Motor Pool reservists.

Bob said that Keith had enjoyed a touch of home when he met a coed from Nebraska in the group. From his area, studying agriculture.

That left me a bit worried and jealous.

After that I had to concentrate on school. During the frantic remainder of the quarter, with reports due and final tests looming, recollection of that welcoming scene relaxed me and warmed my heart all over again. Though the coed from Nebraska did come to mind too.

Suddenly, Christmas came upon us. Without thinking about it, I found myself inviting Keith to join in our family Christmas gathering, after I heard that reserve duties didn't leave him enough time to go back to the Midwest.

With regrets, he declined. He said he didn't want to upset my family's holiday plans, and most of the Motor Pool team as well as other veterans will be stuck here, he said. So we've planned a series of Christmas activities, including Christmas worship at a Lutheran church here.

So we should have a meaningful and joyous holiday…though I'll sure miss you.

As he dropped me off at the train station, he announced that maybe he could drive north before New Year's, and we could come back here together. We do have a staff sedan I can borrow. Besides, I'd

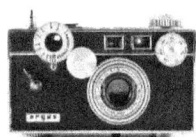

like to check if I can with the Motor Pool there about any news related to the wrecked Cadillac.

Great! I responded, with renewed enthusiasm. And we have a spare bedroom for you.

How about the Hot Rod in the Rose Parade? I asked.

We're not quite ready for show time, said Keith. So we welcome another year of preparation. Maybe our Hot Rod will gain in status as legitimate by that time too.

Swell, but sorry for the delay of the debut for the Hot Rod.

If you can make it, our family and friends look forward to meeting you. And you will enjoy them, I'm sure. They have suspicions about the Cadillac too. And I'll make prints from my double-exposed negatives to see if those photos reveal anything new. Had planned to make enlargements during the Thanksgiving break but didn't get around to it.

Meanwhile, Merry Christmas! to you and all the others!

You too, he said, as he hugged me warmly and firmly.

And Christmas greetings to your family! he added, with a quick goodbye kiss. I sure look forward to seeing you at your place.

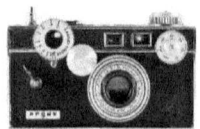

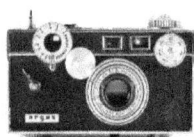

Chapter 24: Welcome to a New Year

For Christmas, we concentrated on worship at our church and greeting others there. At home, we enjoyed lots of food and fellowship. Our usual family and friends participated, but we missed Carla, who had gone back to Madison for the holidays.

We skipped buying presents, because we had agreed again to contribute to those in need, thankful for our own comfortable life.

Bill teased me about the coming visit by Keith. What's he like, besides the photo you showed us?

Like you, Bill. Smart, athletic, kind. Guess I'd call him a typical stoic Scandinavian, I answered.

That we understand, laughed Mom.

Disciplined, you might say. He admitted he quit smoking, but for a pragmatic reason. His earlier Motor Pool, like now, had a paint shop, he explained. But a careless smoker ignited chemicals and lost his life and cost the life of a couple of others. So he kicked the habit, he said.

Good for him, said Mom.

At DuPont, chimed in Dad, we're obviously and continuously concerned about such handling of chemicals. Glad Keith learned an important lesson. Besides, his health will benefit from quitting smoking.

Why did he get involved in your suspicion about the Cadillac wreck? Bill asked.

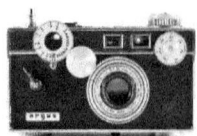

Keith mentioned that he and many other veterans had fumed about civilians making money in the Black Market while the soldiers risked their lives. He said the Black Market also flourishes extensively in Europe—now and well before the end of the war.

I think he welcomes opportunity for possible revenge. Also, it challenges his skills and abilities.

Besides, he said his family in Nebraska reported that their shop has repaired a lot of cars and machinery bought by customers through the Black Market there. The many hazardous defects the garage has had to correct make them mad too.

Keith's not so stoic, after all, smiled Dad.

Three days after Christmas, our neighborhood got a puzzling surprise, when an olive-drab '41 Dodge four-door sedan with Army markings pulled up in front of our house.

Mom saw it first and exclaimed, Here he is!

We knew what that meant, as we went to the front window to watch Keith get out of the car and start up our walkway.

Oh! He is tall and handsome! Mom blurted.

Yes he is! I echoed, and opened the door and met Keith partway up the walk.

He opened his arms and wrapped me in them. And I responded in turn.

So we walked hand in hand to the door and I began introductions.

Seems like we know you already, said Mom.

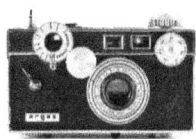

That way to me, too, said Keith, as he shook hands with Mom, Dad and Bill.

Dad whispered to me, Not so stoic after all.

You made it in time for coffee, said Mom.

Counted on it, laughed Keith.

Excuse me, said Keith. I've got something in the car for the occasion.

He came back with a wooden box full of a dozen bottles of wine.

Wine created by our experts in our Motor Pool, he announced. Labeled with their ID. Maybe you'll be willing to be our tasters and testers. Our vintners are eager for reactions.

To go with our dinner, said Mom.

BACKGROUND BRIEFING

The thriving wine industry in California was devastated in 1920, when the 18th Amendment to the U.S. Constitution went into effect to ban alcoholic drinks. That amendment was repealed in 1933 by the 21st Amendment. And the wineries rebounded with vigor, with California again a leading wine producer.

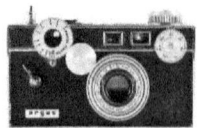

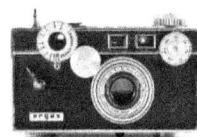

Chapter 25: Futurists

When Mom announced dinner, she also announced she had selected a chardonnay from Keith's wine.

So here's to Keith, she said.

And to all of you, Keith responded. And he winked at me as I lifted my glass, to approve that I was old enough to drink now. At least at home.

After a sip, Bill pronounced it excellent, as he described it in winery terms I didn't know he knew. Thanks so much for this premium product, he said. And keep us posted about when it might be available.

Mom and I brought the turkey and fixin's to go with the array of food already on the table. Dad volunteered to carve and serve.

After a prayer of thanks by Dad, dinner discussion ranged from tomorrow's Rose Bowl game to the activities of us students.

Guess I'd vote for Illinois, said Keith. Bill agreed that UCLA seemed outclassed this year.

Seems like we don't have any rabid California fans in this bunch, concluded Dad.

With Bill on the Stanford team, we kept a close on them, said Dad. Pretty good season, too.

Yeah, 6-3-1, said Bill. Though Sarah claims your team at Santa Barbara did better.

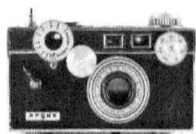

In numbers, maybe, but leagues apart in level of competition, laughed Keith.

You look sturdy enough to be an athlete, Mom said to Keith. Did you play football too?

In high school. Small-time stuff, with 6-man football. Still, the University of Nebraska wanted me. But the draft got me.
Santa Barbara also wanted me for football now, laughed Keith, and a lot of other has-been football veterans.

But most of us wanted to get on with life. Many are married and have families.

I look forward to seeing you play, Bill. Maybe next season in Los Angeles.

I'm curious about your Hot Rod, said Dad as he shifted back to the Rose Parade. Sarah, you gave an enthusiastic report, he said to me. More about the color than the power.

That's my area of interest, too, said Mom. Color, that is, as in art.

Even for us Motor Pool guys, responded Keith, we're proud of the looks of our Rod.

DuPont paint, I hope, said Dad with chuckle.

It is, answered Keith, and who would expect a shade of olive could be so beautiful. Primer and several coats of your paint, our V marking in a shade of yellow, and then some layers of clear coating. Dazzling to look at—as well as dazzling in performance.

It's so pretty, we don't want to enter it in a race. Might get bumped and scraped.

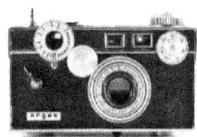

You'll get over that, laughed Bill, when you feel the adrenalin of competition.

I worry also about your dazzling daughter, said Keith as he looked toward my parents, that she might get bumped and scraped in competition too.

How's that? asked Bill.

Because Sarah's being groomed to run for a position next year on the student council, explained Keith.

What's this? inquired Mom.

After our promotional activities to bridge the veterans with the younger students, I explained, many others in my dorm and on the newspaper staff, even some in our English class, started testing the political water.

We veterans got wind of this campaign, so to speak, said Keith, and heartily support Sarah in appreciation for her concern for us. Besides, she's smart and would be an attractive candidate, in more ways than one. Important in politics, of course.

Not a surprising opportunity, said Bill. You had already alerted us, Sarah, about your interests shifting from science to political science. Go for it! I'd say.

As the conversation wound down, I mentioned to Keith that we have a room for him. Good, he said, I had hoped I wouldn't have to sleep in the car. Though I've slept in worse places. I'll get my duffle bag from the car.

I'll go with you, I said.

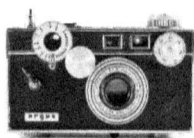

After he snagged his duffle bag from the trunk, he stood right in front of me, then suddenly kissed me.

Fresh! I laughed. Then I kissed him with vigor, and he responded in kind.

Back in the house, he admitted the day had been enjoyable, but long. Taps for me, he said.

What time do you come alive in the morning? he asked.

About 8:00, we can have breakfast while we listen to the description of the Rose Parade, said Dad. You will probably want to visualize your Hot Rod in the parade next year.

Sounds good. See you then, said Keith, as he headed down the hall.

I stayed behind for family discussion. Turned out to be affirmation.

He's a winner, said Bill softly. Mom nodded yes, and Dad signaled thumbs up.

Then we talked more about law study for Bill and political science for me. And politics for me.

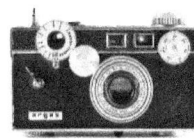

Chapter 26: Bowled Over

Keith said he didn't need reveille to wake up. Habit woke him well before breakfast time, so he had taken his time getting ready.

Nor did he wear military garb. He said he relished being a sort-of civilian again, though the Army still connects with those of us in active reserve. He explained that he enjoyed the benefits of his casual life in the Motor Pool, except for periodic formal training.

Right now, he added, problems related to returning veterans challenge the Army, and education offers an important and valuable option. So we benefit from surprising opportunity and freedom.

At the breakfast table in the kitchen, we all ate heartily and enjoyed the descriptions of the floats and bands in the Rose Parade.

Don't hear about a Hot Rod in the lineup, I commented.

Just wait till next year, countered Keith with a grin.

I hope to see that dazzling DuPont paint, laughed Dad.

It'll be so bright, you'll be able to see your reflection, chuckled Keith. And the Hot Rod will probably be brightened from inside by an aspiring politician, he added as he touched my arm. Pretty girls seem to dominate the Parade, for some reason, he smiled.

By the time the Parade finished, we needed a coffee break, of course, before the preview of the Rose Bowl teams.

Keith reminded us of another reason for his drive north. I hope to contact my Motor Pool counterpart here to see if his team has found and checked your Cadillac.

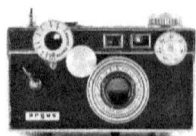

That reminds me, I said, I did make these prints as I promised from my double-exposed negatives of the local parade I mentioned.

You take a look first, Bill, because you'll recognize people who might show despite the double exposure.

Suddenly, Bill looked stunned. Even in this double-exposed scene, he exclaimed, Stan the Con Man shows in the corner of the photo taken before the start of our parade! And at that time he said he was in Fresno!

I came to the same conclusion, I said.

Do these fit in the context with the rest of the negatives? he asked.

Right in the middle, I said.

Something stinks in Denmark! Bill declared.

Sounds that way from what I hear, said Keith. Let me look too.

After I handed him the prints, he recognized the Cadillac convertible I had shown him in a photo before. There's the license that we're searching for.

Dad and Mom were trying to take this in, as they looked at the photos too.

Do you mean to imply that Stan was directly connected with the accident that killed the Moore girl! exclaimed Dad.

Something's sure fishy here, repeated Bill. Maybe Stan the Con Man had actually been driving the car when it flipped, he surmised. Perhaps he was thrown well clear before the car rolled over and he landed in a cushioned roadside. And then disappeared.

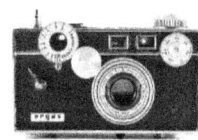

You said, Sarah, that the car developed a shimmy, then a severe shake at high speeds, Keith added.

Yeah, Stan liked to show off, I confirmed. Even scare his passengers with the shaking of the front end.

Maybe he was actually driving that day, showing off too much for Stacy Moore, speculated Bill, and the right front wheel caught the edge of the pavement. And he could have panicked and lost control.

Why did he drive a car with what might have had a damaged front end? puzzled Keith.

It looked beautiful, I said. Maybe that's all he cared about.

Well, if our Motor Pool here can track down that Cadillac and examine it, said Keith, we might have some answers.

And I'm going to bring this up with our study group at the law school, said Bill.

I hate to jump to conclusions about Stan, he continued, but that conniving son of a bitch might have been involved in criminal negligence.

I guess we can let this rest for now, hoping your guys, Keith, can find evidence. Meanwhile, we have to keep these photos and negatives safely stored, concluded Bill.

I'll see to that, said my frowning Dad. I'll put them in our safe-deposit box at the bank.

He seemed like such a pleasant and honorable young man, said my perplexed mother.

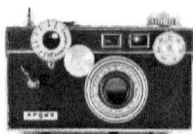

When he wanted to put on a good front for whatever purpose, I said.

His showing off put many others at risk, surmised Dad.

This time, it appears, his dishonesty plus his showing off may have caused the death of an innocent person.

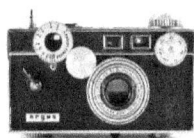

Chapter 27: Forensics

The next day, Keith contacted his Motor Pool colleague in the Bay Area.

If it's okay with you, Keith, I'll get on the other line, said Bill. He introduced himself as a law student at Stanford.

Later, Keith and Bill summarized the grim but revealing phone report.

Those guys in the Motor Pool unit here know their stuff, and their geography, said Keith. After boiling their inquiry down to one wrecking yard, they pinned down our Cadillac.

Using their Uncle Sam authority, they have had the car impounded in a fenced area of the wrecking yard so it can't be moved without military approval. Specifically, approval by my Army Motor Pool colleague.

Meanwhile, he has arranged to take photos over, around and under.

He will send me a set and another here, said Keith.

The Cadillac remains in surprisingly good shape, he had reported, except for the flattened windshield, of course.

He did mention a puzzle that had him scratching his head. Didn't you say a woman was driving? he had asked.

Yes, that's what we were told.

She must have been tall, he said, because the driver's seat was set way back.

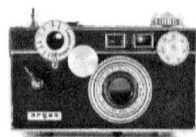

Bill informed him that he thought Stacy was about 5 foot 6. So the puzzle remained.

Now the big news, the Army colleague continued. We think, he reported, we might have discovered the cause of the accident.

The connecting rod for the steering system was badly bent. This accident could have caused that, but the damage looks older. The bent rod caused excessive wear on the linkage too. Also, the wear on the front tires confirms the bad alignment. Sure would have shimmied, even at low speed. Hate to think of the higher-speed consequences.

We took lots of photos underneath the front end, he explained. Started by photographing the way we first saw that steering area, then after we washed it clean.

The rest of the way underneath seemed okay, he concluded.

Keith and Bill had thanked him for the great work and for the report. We might call on you again as this investigation progresses.

Where do we go from here with this information? pondered Bill.

Probably, said Dad, to seek an opportunity to review the police report about the accident. Find out what Stan said about when and where he was. And will that report list the steering damage?

Well, as I mentioned before, said Bill, I need to tell about the accident to my law study group for analysis. Maybe also to the law professor who is the group's advisor.

Puzzling. The photo shows Stan barely visible at the ceremony.

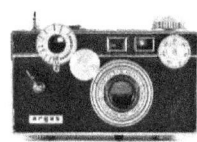

The seat position in the Cadillac. Might he have been driving after all, but was thrown away from the rollover? Injured?

Did he go to Fresno and how might he have gone?

Terrible! said Mom. The death of Stacy. Now possible implications of Stan.

Unfortunately, the wheeling and dealing seem to go on at all levels of life, Dad philosophized. Stan, and maybe his family, evidently bends the rules to satisfy self-importance and greed. Now we may be personally seeing the consequences of those weaknesses.

I still feel guilt about Stacy's death, I admitted. A bad ending however this evolves.

BACKGROUND BRIEFING

The Black Market was rampant in the war zones of Europe, but also occurred in America. Such transactions tend to be illegal, so the Black Market must operate outside the conventional economic system to sell contraband goods, avoid taxes and skirt price controls. And earn hefty profits.

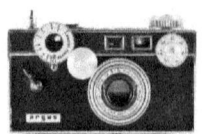

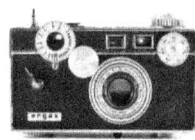

Chapter 28: Reflective Return

Chivalry isn't dead, I laughed, as Keith opened the door for me, after we put our luggage in the trunk.

Sir Galahad at your service, he grinned.

I waved out the car window till we got to the end of the block and my family in front of the house was out of view.

Great folks, he said as he saw me waving. Lucky you, he added. And lucky me, for their friendship. And for my friendship with their daughter.

We do seem to be good for each other, I said. You're helping me grow in maturity and purpose. And affection, I added as I touched his arm

Thanks to you, and to your family, I seem to be edging beyond my attachment to the memory of Karina. And the involvement of you and your friends in our Hot Rod adds a lot of enjoyment to that project.

We certainly benefit from visiting your Motor Pool, I said. Fun and interesting for me, and the others. Plus delicious food.

Then I switched to being a tour guide, as I announced and explained the landmarks and other highlights of our drive south. Going past Salinas, I mentioned the importance of John Steinbeck, whose literature fit in our English class.

Hard not to get caught up in the trials and tragedies of the Great Depression as depicted in *Grapes of Wrath*, said Keith. We had it tough a lot of times in Nebraska, but we could scrape out a living

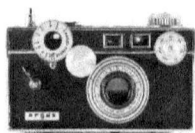

even in the worst of times. We had a big garden and we fixed and made things ourselves.

I admitted that we had it easier, with my dad an important technical representative of DuPont and Mom a teacher. But we heard about skimping by others and we talked about the challenges of the Great Depression.

I particularly admire the photo-journalism about the Depression by Dorthea Lange—from our area, like Steinbeck. Both created widespread awareness of the plight of the destitute.

Of course, the war caused a major migration west for jobs in the defense industry.

Later, Keith commented about the beauty of our home, so I told about the architectural influence of Bernard Maybeck. He created the big structures, I explained, but many other builders followed the basic characteristics of his designs. Warm and friendly, I added.

Makes me think of our big old house in Nebraska, he said quietly.

You must miss your home and family, I offered.

After the war, I visited home briefly. Then the Army sent me here, followed by starting college. A long distance and long time away, he said. But a fulfilling new life, he added. Can't go home again, to quote one of the writers we've studied.

Yeah, I agreed, Thomas Wolfe captures that feeling—probably more for you than me.

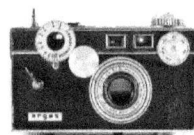

We rolled south quietly, perhaps both of us thinking about how we got acquainted by the accident of the alphabet. And how that accident has led to an interesting and supportive relationship.

There's our supply store, grinned Keith, as we went past the vast array of Army vehicles and equipment at Camp Roberts. I have to report here occasionally for training, whenever the Army has time for it. The glut of soldiers and equipment dominates life here. I think the officers gladly let us stay self-sufficient at our niche in the military air base at Goleta, while they run the regular Army.

Countless soldiers await their discharge. Then, for those veterans, getting jobs or going to school will be their next big challenge.

I admitted that the Army situation surprised me. I think most of us just feel relief that the war is over, without realizing the impact of the shift to peacetime.

An understandable reaction, said Keith. Hard to believe my good fortune of getting a fresh start.

I hope the world gets a fresh start too with the creation of the new United Nations, said Keith. I remember discussions and disappointments in our family about the hopes for the earlier League of Nations. It failed to live up to its good intentions. My parents expressed similar regret that the Kellogg-Brian Pact had been intended to outlaw war—but didn't succeed, of course.

As we passed Camp San Luis, Keith offered a casual salute. Then we passed the town of San Luis Obispo. Our Chefs are working closely with some specialists here at Cal Poly, he said. Good connection. Good wine!

Dusk had set in by the time we reached my dorm at Santa Barbara. Glad to be home, said Keith, though I already miss your family.

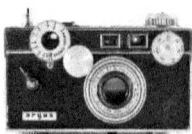

Me too.

Don't think we'll be sitting next to each other this quarter, I said. But I thank the luck of the alphabet for putting us together.

With that, he wrapped his arms around me and kissed me gently. And I responded not so gently.

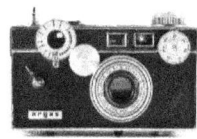

Chapter 29: More Reflections

Our alphabetic connection ended at the conclusion of that English class, though Keith and I still saw each other on campus occasionally.

We got together once in a while for coffee, and he did invite me to an unusual gathering for a movie. The Army had acquired a supply of Geodesic Domes that were now surplus. So the college community of veterans and their families had snagged one and erected it for a community center, not far from the Motor Pool buildings.

BACKGROUND BRIEFING

Like the military's Quonset Hut with its curved steel components easily assembled as a semi-cylinder, the Geodesic Dome featured triangular units that could be put together to form a semi-dome. Both the half-cylinder Quonset and the half-sphere Geodesic Dome offered open and unsupported space suited to many military uses.

Keith mentioned that a former chaplain conducted Sunday worship services there. Maybe we can take that in some Sunday, he added.

The community center also offers a lot of recreational and learning options, he explained, including a setup for movies.

So it was a great treat when Keith asked me to go with him to the movie *Going My Way* at the community center.

Bing Crosby sure helped boost morale during the war, he said, and I'm looking forward to seeing him in an unusual role as a priest.

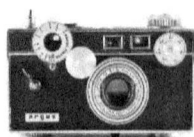

So am I, said I.

Dinner too, he added. Our Chefs look forward to showing off their culinary talents.

And I look forward to seeing your Motor Pool bunch again. And your Hot Rod.

I have another surprise for you, announced Keith. Our Motor Pool is helping restore a military Piper Cub. Not just an ordinary one, but a special military model, called the Super Cub. Better visibility. Bigger engine, speed up to 130 miles per hour and a range up to 460 miles.

It should be ready for action by next fall. It's a trainer—room for both of us. I'll learn to fly it. Then teach you, too.

Dream on! I responded.

Now, he said, the rebuilding of the plane is coming along, with lots of specialists welcoming the challenge. Of course, we do have ample surplus planes nearby to scrounge from.

When it looks presentable, we'll arrange for show and tell.

Then later maybe we can fly up to the Bay Area. Moffett Field still serves the Army, so we could land there. The Cub will have enough range for one way, with a fill-up for the return. Then easy reach to your home from Moffett.

With the Cub's slow pace, you could even try some aerial photography.

Sure, I laughed, all this after you've proven your flying skill.

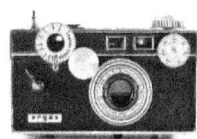

Oh, we could have parachutes along, just in case, he grinned.

For our present outing, Keith arrived with his chariot, the motorcycle and side-car. Going my way? he asked.

We'd like to go with you, laughed several onlookers.

The whole evening proved to be a delight. The dinner. The movie. And getting acquainted with the families as well as the single student-veterans who came for the movie. Women student-veterans made up part of the movie crowd, including some nurses going back to college to expand their capabilities.

Keith later said that seeing and meeting the nurses did cause him a sad pang of remembrance. He did mention that he tries to stay in touch with Karina's family to keep the memory of her alive.

Still, the joy of the event prevailed as he took me back to the dorm.

Of course, talk from side-car to the motorcycle proved to be impossible, not to mention any possibilities for romantic sharing.

But students with a view of my arrival did clap and cheer when Keith kissed me as he helped me out of the side-car.

The grapevine beat me in sharing my experience with the *El Gaucho* staff.

After we laughed about my dramatic coming and going, we then realized that the movies for the community of veterans and families serves as another way of bridging the campus groups.

Maybe, said Bob, you could wangle an invitation for us to visit that community.

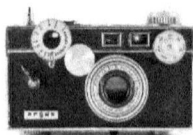

Seems do-able, I said.

Good! he grinned. I count on your persuasive style.

And so it came to pass. The folks at the community of veterans and families welcomed a chance to build a stronger link to the college.

And the recreation leaders suggested a repeat of Bing Crosby, along with Ingrid Bergman, in *The Bells of Saint Mary's.* Keith, of course, looked forward to seeing and hearing Bing again. And so did our staff. And so did the many among the veterans with fond memories of hearing Bing during the war.

This time, Bob assigned me to write a story and take photos of the gathering. Another important step in unifying the college, he declared.

Why don't we start our own tour of Hollywood for the folks here? I wondered in a staff meeting.

Then the others, more knowledgeable than I about Hollywood, chimed in. For the families, a tour could help acquaint them about their new home area. Learn a lot and have fun. For us, too!

Before long, an Army bus became a tour bus, making a series of tourist runs so everyone in the community got a chance.

The route ran from Griffith Park, the zoo, past the Hollywood sign, stopping at a movie lot, even meeting some patriotic stars. Then on past homes of some of those stars in Beverly Hills, finally overwhelming a new outdoor restaurant with our massive order of hamburgers, French fries and root beer.

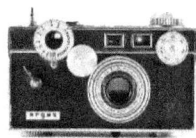

As I reflected about the tours, an idea popped into my head. Maybe Mom and Dad and Janet and her parents would enjoy getting in on a tour. Learn a lot. Have fun too. Even add an art museum for Mom.

And they would meet some interesting young families.

Bill, of course, would no doubt get his own special tour when his Stanford team plays in Los Angeles. Lucky him!

As the word spread about our connection with the veterans' village, college leaders informed us at the *El Gaucho* of their appreciation for this step forward in relationships.

Like the maturing influence of Keith and his Motor Pool, the community of veterans and their families helped me move toward a more balanced life.

At last!

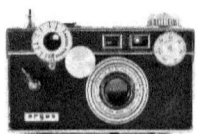

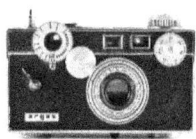

Chapter 30: Parting, Connecting

The remainder of my successful school year flew by, and I regretted saying farewell, especially to Keith and to the staff of *El Gaucho*, not to mention my dorm-mates.

Thanks to *El Gaucho,* my classes and the photo club, my photo-journalism skills had increased steadily. So I looked forward to working again for our hometown newspaper during the summer.

Then, with the help of Bill, I could continue to investigate the Cadillac tragedy and its consequences.

I also vowed to myself I'd renew acquaintance with Ron Hanson and get an update about his Hot Rod.

With his automotive knowledge, he might serve as an expert regarding the Cadillac. And perhaps we could work together in promoting his and Keith's Hot Rods.

Keith said Army reserve training would take up most of his summer, but maybe he'd have time to visit his family in Nebraska. My Nebraska friend invited me to visit her and her family in Lincoln, he explained.

But later in the summer, I will try to drive up your way again too.

I hope so, I smiled.

During one of the last gatherings at the veterans' community, he and I danced to the music of Glenn Miller. And Keith said that the mysterious disappearance of Glenn Miller over the English Channel

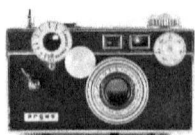

saddened him and a lot of other GI's, not to mention those on the home-front who cherished his music too.

Strange, pondered Keith. Glenn Miller died about the same time the Battle of the Bulge began. Then, a few months later, President Roosevelt died.

The President had handled enormous challenges with courage and determination—at least most people, and most soldiers, felt that way.

We worried about how our new President would face the challenges, recalled Keith. Well, he authorized the atom bombs to finally end the war.

What next? Keith wondered aloud. We were strange bedfellows with the Soviet Union. Now we worry about how Uncle Joe Stalin will try to control the peace. But I think our plain-spoken President Truman will push back.

Sorry the world is such a mess, I said, as my hand found his.

Later, warm weather welcomed a bunch of us to go to the beach, though the Pacific Ocean never does get warm. Always great scenery though. And practically part of our campus.

The Chefs served up some great food again. They had been working with food specialists from Cal Poly, who also came by for a taste, so to speak, of our beach party. Naturally, they brought some of their concoctions from their Best in the West.

All good things must come to an end, it seems. Or at least a pause. So once again, Keith and his Jeep took me to the train station, where we shared an affectionate farewell.

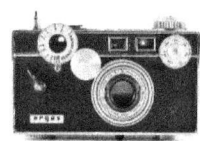

And, once again, Mom and Dad and the Volvo met me at my station. For an affectionate reunion.

BACKGROUND BRIEFING

Volvo began making cars 1927, at its factory in Gothenburg, Sweden. *Volvo* means *I roll* in Latin, which relates to the company's development and manufacturing of ball bearings. Volvo founders aimed to build cars to withstand the rigors of Sweden's rough roads and cold temperatures. That Volvo reputation spread to America after World War II.

They beamed with happiness as I told them about my growth as a student, photo-journalist and as a maturing person.

Mom revealed their plan for a collegiate reunion, before Carla's return to Wisconsin. In fact, said Dad, Bill plans to chauffeur her home in our Volvo. Check in with friends and family on the way.

And Janet and her family again will join in our gathering.

Earlier, Mom reminded me, you mentioned wanting to learn more about Ron's Hot Rod. Why don't you get in touch with him. He's really a delightful guy, active in our church and smart as a whip.

So I called him, and he said he would gladly share information about his Hot Rod, and he expressed keen interest in our Hot Rod. And the publicity possibilities.

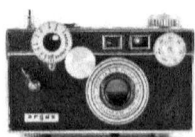

He took me up on my invitation to visit at our house on a Saturday afternoon, so all of us could learn about his Hot Rod hobby. In fact, he drove up in his Hot Rod.

Of course, we all gathered around his toy. Beautiful, said Mom, as she admired its lines and colors. Ron assured Dad that the glistening paint had come from DuPont.

Bill quizzed him about the power and performance.

And I visualized the publicity potential. I also realized that plain and quiet Ron had grown to be tall and good looking. And quite charming.

He proudly pointed out the colorful design on both sides of his Hot Rod. For you, he said, in honor of your Pacific paradise. So, instead of the often-featured waves of flame on Hot Rods, Ron's art depicted a wave of surf in dazzling shades of blue and white.

Hey Ron, I exclaimed, you should connect with the Art Center School of Design in Los Angeles. Noted for industrial design. Especially cars. I hope to visit there some time to learn more about the photography department there. I heard that Ansel Adams taught there at one time.

Let's go! he laughed. Show off our Hot Rod, too. Someday, anyway.

Then Ron mentioned that he had heard about our investigation of the Cadillac rollover that killed Stacy. Still sad to think about it, he said. In various ways, we all expressed our sorrow.

The rollover does seem strange, he said. If I can help figure out how that could have happened, let me know. For engineering credit, I've

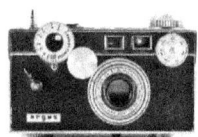

done a lot of study of various aspects of steering and handling, he added.

Good, responded Bill. That's one of the puzzles, along with a few other questions we have. Such as legal responsibilities related to repaired cars. We've pondered that question in our Stanford group that's analyzing the issue, including how to start a new official inquiry.

My dad's a trial lawyer, said Ron, and he might be able to provide some advice. I think I could persuade him to offer pro bono participation, he laughed.

And we think we've found some contradictions regarding Stan's involvement, explained Bill.

Stan's sure a sleaze, responded Ron. Oops! Sorry, he said, as he looked at me. Hope he wasn't your boyfriend.

Just enamored of his car, I laughed.

You'll appreciate Keith, my new special friend from college. Definitely not a sleaze. He's an engineering student and leader of an Army reserve unit he calls the Motor Pool. They're building a Hot Rod as part of unofficial Army research. And the Army hopes it will build good public relations, too. Maybe even enter it in the Rose Parade next year.

Wow! You've got my attention! exclaimed Ron. Tell me more.

I've got quite a bunch of photos. I'll get them out for show and tell on another day.

Speaking of another day, said Ron, I'd better get going. Taken enough of your time already.

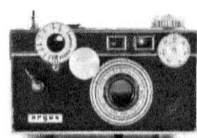

Only after you've tasted my dessert and savored my coffee, said Mom.

Sure to be good, I added. I think she got the recipe from the Motor Pool I mentioned. Two of the reservists are students and focus on food management, so they come up with some great stuff.

Bring it on, said Dad. I like the flavor of motor oil in my dessert, he laughed. And we laughed with him.

And I felt a tug of longing for Keith.

Now, Ron announced later, I think I'm fueled up to hit the road. So we all went out for another look at his Rod.

Then, he surprised me. Want to take a spin?

Well…sure, I answered, hesitantly.

Hop in, he said as he held the door for me.

This is a Model B pickup, he explained. For picking up girls, he laughed, as did the rest of my family. And I had to laugh with them.

During supper, our family reviewed the pleasure of getting better acquainted with Ron.

Great guy, said Bill with a snicker, considering he goes to our arch rival Cal.

Maybe we'll get some valuable legal help from his dad, too.

How was your test drive, asked Dad.

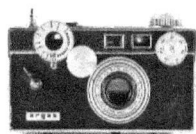

Fun, I answered. And exciting, the way he maneuvered through our neighborhood. Shifting up, then down, gunning the engine out of sharp curves.

Within the speed limit, of course.

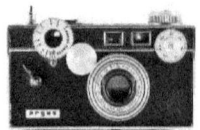

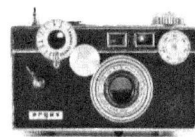

Chapter 31: Next Moves

As we analyzed the Cadillac case, Bill suggested some legal options. Could nail Stan with perjury, criminal negligence and leaving the scene of an accident. Was his family also in on a possible cover-up? Bill wondered.

We could start by asking to re-open the inquiry about the rollover, he added. We should have enough new evidence. The photos showing Stan at the start of the parade when he said he was in Fresno. The record of pre-existing damage to the steering, and testimony about the shimmying and shaking of the car.

Now that he had joined our truth squad, Ron offered to seek an opinion from his dad about the importance of the new material and how to reopen the case.

Ron, could you see if your dad would take the first steps? asked Bill.

No doubt officials in the justice system won't respond quickly, speculated Bill. That should allow time for Carla and me to make a round trip to the Midwest. Then our truth squad could be back in action before college starts for all of us.

Seems reasonable, we concluded. And Ron agreed to launch the first step.

A couple days later Ron called me to report about the enthusiastic involvement of his dad in our case. And he would start the ball rolling regarding a review of the Cadillac accident inquiry.

While I've got you on the line, continued Ron, I want to recruit you to be in our community's summer-stock play. A musical called *Kiss Me, Kate*. Know that story?

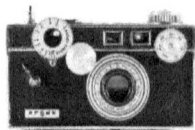

Oh yes, I laughed. I got a certain self-awareness from that—based on Shakespeare's *The Taming of the Shrew*. Helped me look back at my shrewish self. Hope I've grown past that.

Well, he said, a bit abashed, you certainly seem more than just good looking. For one thing, I remember from church your good voice, which would fit this casual musical. Of course, with your sharp memory, you could learn your lines in no time at all. And maybe help me get a part too.

Want to take a spin to look over the store-front theater? asked Ron. Fits the amateurish nature of the production.

Sure. When?

We should aim to be there tomorrow afternoon, about 2:00. The director and a few players will be there for a meeting. Pick you up about 1:30.

You're determined to pick me up, aren't you, I chuckled.

You've got me pegged, he laughed.

The next day, off we went in Ron's Hot Rod. The production staff and some of the actors welcomed us.

Ron assured me you can sing, said the director. He sure can sing, so I consider him a good judge.

Of character, too? I asked. Because I'm emerging from my shrew shell, I laughed.

Yep, Ron vouched for you. And that's good enough for us.

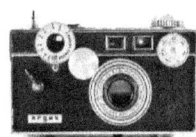

Then I met the lead performers and got an overview of the story and the roles of the support players. Then the pianist went through selections of the main numbers, with the featured singers joining in. Next, Ron and I learned about the minor roles we would fill. Ron easily got in the groove, but I needed time to get in the swing of my small part. A bit rusty, I admitted.

Sounded right on, said the director. Just take your time to get the feel for your part.

Later, I joked with Ron that he sure gambled in betting on my singing.

I counted on your voice, and your parents had told me how you have developed as a college leader. Sounds like a thespian to me, he laughed.

And I laughed too—about the word thespian.

Want to drive? he asked on our way out of the theater.

You do like to gamble, I laughed again. At least I know manual shifting. And I sure would like to test your pct.

On the way home, he coached me about the gears and the positive steering response. Not like the marshmallow feel of most cars, he explained.

Pull over here, he then said, and ease into that parking space.

Then I realized we had stopped in front of a malt shop.

I think we should celebrate our shot at acting fame, he chuckled. Want a malt?

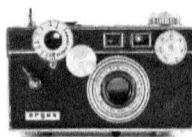

Great idea!

Gradually we became a two-some. In the theater, at the swimming pool, on the tennis court—and in the Hot Rod.

When cousin Janet called about dropping by for a visit, she kidded again about my lining her up with a cute guy.

I thought you hooked up with a lumberjack at college, I reminded her.

Well, we agreed that we should have some fun apart from each other this summer, she dithered. He in Minnesota, me here.

How about you? she questioned.

Sort of the same, I admitted, with a sense of disloyalty. Nebraska instead of your Minnesota.

Later, Ron declared that he had just the right guy for Janet. Jeff Johnson. Also from our church. An agricultural student at Cal Poly. Smart and fun. Not bad looking either. Home for the summer.

I admitted that I vaguely remembered him from church, but not from school.

He was quiet and studious, said Ron. Not the kind to get attention from you cheerleaders.

He grew a lot in one year at college, said Ron. More outgoing now. Even cheerleaders might find him appealing.

Sounds like a good candidate for Janet, I said. Double date, double fun.

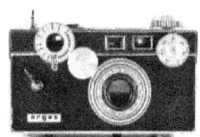

When I opened door for our dates, I almost lost my voice from the surprise. Ron and Jeff looked almost like twins. Truly a double date, I thought.

Not related, said Ron. Except maybe way back among the Vikings, he chuckled.

Then surprise left him almost speechless. Twins? he asked when he saw me and Janet together.

Looks like a double-double date, he said.

Janet and I are just cousins, I laughed. But we do confuse people.

That includes me, he said, as he greeted Janet and introduced Jeff to both of us. Then my parents came from the living room to greet Ron and Jeff.

They too did a double-take, and Mom mentioned she recognized Jeff as well as Ron from church.

Is this one of your double-exposures, Sarah? chuckled Dad, as he went on to explain the connection to my camera.

Embarrassed, I suggested we be on our way to the movie.

What movie, asked curious Mom.

Ron recommends a new musical called *Till the Clouds Roll By.*

With its enjoyable songs, it should warm up me and Ron for our cameo singing appearance in the local stage musical *Kiss Me, Kate.*

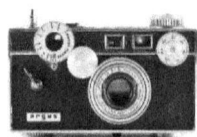

BACKGROUND BRIEFING

Till the Clouds Roll By was a movie musical made in 1946 by MGM. The film is a fictionalized biography of composer Jerome Kern (who was originally involved with the production of the film, but died before it was completed). The movie featured stars such as singer Judy Garland and actor Van Heflin.

Where's your Hot Rod? asked Janet when we went out the door.

Had to borrow the family station wagon to hold all of us, admitted Ron.

What, no rumble seat in your Hot Rod? Janet jokingly inquired. Would have been cozy for Sarah and me. Or me and Jeff.

Sorry, but you wouldn't want to ride in the back. I made my Hot Rod out of a pickup truck.

He claims, I said, that he uses the pickup to pick up girls.

Like us, giggled Janet.

Jeff just smiled at the banter.

Our casual summer romances would continue until time for all of us to go back to college.

After Bill and Carla got back from the Midwest, they reported about their travel adventures, including visits with our relatives and Carla's family. All of the folks we connected with are proud of us,

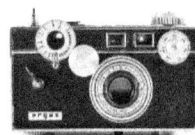

and we felt the same about them, Bill reported. Including, of course, Carla's parents, he added.

Carla doesn't go back to Stanford for a few days. Hope she can stay here, he said to Mom and Dad, while I head for football practice.

Be delighted, said Mom. And Dad and I heartily agreed

By the way, Dad, the Volvo runs like a Swiss watch. Well, a Swedish watch

Before Bill left for Stanford football practice, he wondered about the status of the Cadillac case. I explained that Ron had convinced his dad to get involved. Pro bono.

So Carla joined our foursome through the lingering summer days.

Hope I'm not a fifth wheel, she said.

The more the merrier, I assured her.

Janet and Jeff developed a shared interest in agriculture, from forests to vineyards, to start a continuing friendship.

Hot Rods bonded me and Ron.

Meanwhile, the other three coached us two thespians and cheered us in our roles in the summer-stock production of *Kiss Me, Kate.*

And I left my shrewish behavior behind for good.

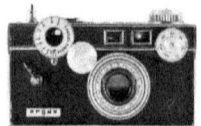

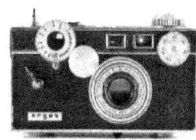

Chapter 32: Still More Moves

Unofficial family-court deliberations about the Cadillac case had begun shortly after Bill returned from the Midwest.

What next? Bill wondered, as he answered his own question by suggesting we meet with Mr. Hanson.

When we met, Mr. Hanson commended us for our pursuit of justice. Your evidence and testimony support a call for a new look at the earlier inquiry, he said. Might result in conviction for vehicular manslaughter based on reckless behavior leading to death, as in this case.

If a court reviews Stan's previous inquiry and he is convicted of vehicular manslaughter, what's the punishment? Bill asked.

Worst case, said Mr. Hanson, could be 15 years to life in prison. But a judge might see mitigating circumstances, such as first offense. Could reduce the sentence to a fine and probation.

Initial action would depend on the involvement of a prosecutor. I could check that, said Mr. Hanson.

Our first step, suggested Bill, would be to poll our own informal jury about what we want to happen. Maybe just to scare Stan and his father to stop their Black Market business.

Publicity, or a threat of publicity, could also have significant impact, I said.

We'll convene our ad hoc jury, said Bill. Then, Mr. Hanson, we will let you know our intention. Again, we thank you for your advice, with hope you will help us through any next steps.

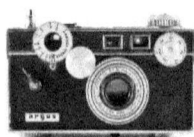

I should have said this before, said Mr. Hanson, with a chuckle, but you can just call me Russ. We might have to be formal in the courtroom, but not among us friends.

So we polled our own informal jury from family and friends, including Keith as represented by me.

Despite our anger about the death of Stacy and about the arrogance and dishonesty of Stan and his father, we deliberated carefully, knowing the extent of possible punishment. We eventually agreed to ask Russ to confer with a prosecutor and the judge who had ruled after the earlier inquest.

Based on the prints from my double-exposed photos and the report and photos from the Bay Area Motor Pool, the prosecutor and the judge agreed that the case could be moved from a simple accident report to indictment of Stan for leaving the scene of a major accident, plus vehicular manslaughter. They also thought the case should include consideration of possible perjury by Stan and his father for false testimony. And they agreed that state authorities should investigate Stan and his father for selling vehicles with hidden damage.

Great work! Bill exclaimed later.

And I commended all involved in our push for an investigation. Won't bring back Stacy, but may at least discourage the lying and chicanery in the Black Market.

Well, we have a ways to go, summarized Bill. Don't know what will happen if a court should convict Stan as well as his father. I'll check with my law-study team for a prediction.

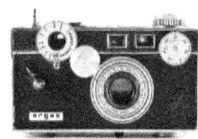

Chapter 33: Trial by Publicity

When the district attorney got the official statement about the case, that office soon buzzed with interest. Several attorneys still felt frustration that the earlier inquiry into the death of Stacy Moore had proved nothing—except to blacken the Black Market reputation of the Logan family.

After the attorneys sought earlier police records, the news of the possible legal action somehow leaked to the news media.

At that time, the investigators recalled, unhappy Black Market customers had complained. But they had to accept *buyer beware* because they eagerly bought Black Market cars and equipment in short supply.

Now the prosecutors saw another chance for redemption by re-opening the case.

The local newspaper pounced on the story first, as some of the staff felt Stan Logan had taken advantage of me, Sarah Karlstrom, as a high school student when I was one of the newspaper's part-time staffers. Reporters felt that Stan's involvement in the death of Stacy Moore remained hazy, though not enough evidence called for conviction at the time.

Larger newspapers and radio stations, previously stewing about the Black Market operating while the country suffered through war, also sensed a chance at redemption by exposing a Black Market enterprise.

Now information leaked that new evidence had surfaced. Such as photos that contradicted Stan Logan's testimony at the inquiry. The Cadillac in question had not been repaired as reputed by the Logan

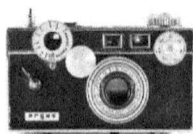

Company, and could have caused the driver to lose control of the car. The question about who drove the car again got attention. Meanwhile, the Logans weren't just sitting on their hands. They had retained a noted defense attorney.

Right away, he attacked the media for trying to convict his client with publicity, including publishing of letters to the editor with complaints about the Logan Company.

He charged the media with the use of the pejorative term Black Market to defame his client.

When Bill came home for the weekend, he reported the reactions of his law-study group.

At least, he said, they had concluded that the threat of a trial might have exposed a sleazy Black Market business. Maybe it will cause claims for recovery of purchase payments made to the Logan Company, and perhaps even put the Logan Company out of business. The Logans' insurance company might also want a reversal of their payment for the Cadillac and the compensation for the death of Stacy Moore.

But in their own mock trial, my law study group questioned the significance of my double-exposed photos showing Stan in contradiction to his testimony at the earlier inquest. The placement of the driver's seat in the Cadillac might have occurred as a consequence of the rollover. And how might Stan have escaped injury if he was ejected from the car. Had any witnesses before verified his whereabouts—or had even been willing to testify? Was the purported structural damage to the steering relevant to such a serious accident? And might the accident have caused the damage?

The prosecutors in the District Attorney office had explored the case in a similar way. Reluctantly, they concluded that they lacked

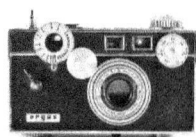

sufficient and credible evidence to convict. And the District Attorney added his assessment of the time and cost of trial. Though not personally convinced, he admitted to the judge that the office would have to drop the case because of insufficient and questionable evidence. An attempt at prosecution could be just a waste of taxpayer money, he said.

With that announcement, the Logans and their defense attorney proclaimed to the news media that justice had been done. But the news media offered little coverage of that statement.

Community interest in and support of the previously esteemed wealthy Logans faded away.

And a barrage of letters to the editor exposed the Logans to further examples of their dishonesty.

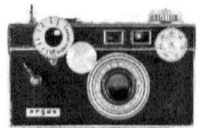

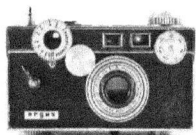

Chapter 34: Poetic Justice

Keith did drive up from Santa Barbara for the start of school.

Then he and other students and parents gathered for farewells at our place.

In fact, we clustered around Ron's Hot Rod, with Keith admiring the pickup. And the rest of us saying our sad goodbyes.

Watch out! Bill suddenly shouted with a shocked warning. That careening tow truck is heading our way and seems out of control!

Then the tow truck skidded within inches of Ron's Hot Rod, and Stan staggered out of the truck.

You bitch! he shouted at me, as he lurched toward me. You've ruined me, you slut, and our company too.

I jumped back when he started to swing at me, but Keith grabbed Stan's arm and twisted him into muttering submission.

Then we heard a siren. A city police car roared our way at high speed.

After the patrol car skidded to a stop, two officers jumped out. With a sense of the situation, they recognized disheveled Stan being controlled by Keith.

One of your neighbors called, said an officer, about a driver racing and swerving in a Logan Company truck that nearly side-swiped the neighbor's car.

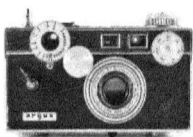

We saw your attempt to control the reckless driver as we approached. Hope no one was hurt.

Not unless I broke the arm of this jerk, said Keith.

Well, Stan, declared the officer with a sense of satisfaction, looks like we'll finally get a delayed verdict about you.

And you can't deny this, he added.

Oh yeah! sputtered Stan. Our family has beaten worse problems than this!

Yeah, we know plenty about you and your reputation and your family, said the officer. This time we'll be glad to testify about your typical aggressive driving—under the influence of booze too.

So, Stan, seems that it's high time you get your delayed day in court! blurted the other officer.

Not just drunk driving, either, he announced as he glared in Stan's face. Attempted battery too.

Even threatening an officer, when you tried take a swing at me.

And, Stan, plenty of witnesses this time, too!

END 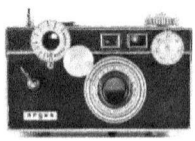 of the Beginning

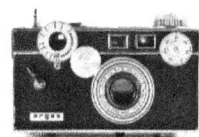

BACKGROUND OF THE CAST

- *Sarah Karlstrom*, student narrator of this story; parents James and Christine, brother Bill

- Sarah's cousin *Janet Karlstrom* and her parents Paul and Emily

- *Stan Logan*, high school classmate of Sarah and part of family involved in the Black Market

- *Keith Kragstad*, World War II veteran, classmate of Sarah at Santa Barbara College

- *Ron Hanson*, Sarah's acquaintance from church and school, creator of his own Hot Rod

- *Bob Felp*, editor of Santa Barbara College student newspaper

- Other military veterans in the college and community, Sarah's college roommates, professors, administrators, media folks

www.ingramcontent.com/pod-product-compliance
Lightning Source LLC
Chambersburg PA
CBHW051313170526
45166CB00002B/526